GoodFood

D0280521

101 MEALS FOR TWO

First published 2006
Published by BBC Books, an imprint of Ebury Publishing
A Random House Group company

20 19 18 17 16 15

Photographs © BBC Magazines 2006
Recipes © BBC Magazines 2006
Book design © Woodlands Books Ltd 2006
All the recipes contained in this book first appeared in
BBC *Good Food* magazine.

The Random House Group Limited Reg. No 954009

Addresses for companies within the Random House Group can be
found at www.randomhouse.co.uk

A CIP catalogue record for this book is available from the British Library.

The Random House Group Limited supports the Forest Stewardship
Council (FSC), the leading international forest certification organization.
All our titles that are printed on Greenpeace approved FSC paper carry
the FSC logo. Our paper procurement policy can be found at
www.rbooks.co.uk/environment

To buy books by your favourite authors and to register for offers visit
www.rbooks.co.uk

Commissioning Editor: Sarah Reece
Project Editor: Laura Nickoll
Designer: Kathryn Gammon
Production: Arlene Alexander

Set in Bookman Old Style and Helvetica
Printed by Firmengruppe APPL, aprinta druck, Wemding, Germany
Colour origination by Dot Gradations Ltd, UK

ISBN 978 0 563 52299 7

GoodFood

101 MEALS FOR TWO
TRIED-AND-TESTED RECIPES

Editor
Angela Nilsen

BOOKS

Contents

Introduction   6

Introduction

Cooking for two is just as rewarding as cooking for four or more – often even more so. The jobs can be shared and you can enjoy preparing the meal together. With more and more requests for recipes for fewer people, we at *BBC Good Food Magazine* thought how useful it would be to put together a collection of specially designed recipes for two, all tried and tested in the Good Food kitchen for ease, simplicity and taste.

You'll find this book packed with ideas to help you plan meals for different scenarios. Perhaps you have something special to celebrate and plan a cosy evening in together? Then there are those days when you want to share something light and healthy, or need inspiration for a quick snack, or something equally simple but more substantial after a day at work, such as *Lamb with Lemon and Dill*, pictured opposite (see page 112 for the recipe) .

To make it easy to plan nutritionally well-balanced meals, each recipe comes with its own calorie count and essential nutritional breakdown.

So when it's just the two of you – go on, cook something different and spoil yourselves.

Angela Nilsen
BBC Good Food Magazine

Conversion tables

NOTES ON THE RECIPES
• Eggs are medium in the UK and Australia (large in America) unless stated otherwise.
• Wash all fresh produce before preparation.

OVEN TEMPERATURES

Gas	°C	Fan °C	°F	Oven temp.
¼	110	90	225	Very cool
½	120	100	250	Very cool
1	140	120	275	Cool or slow
2	150	130	300	Cool or slow
3	160	140	325	Warm
4	180	160	350	Moderate
5	190	170	375	Moderately hot
6	200	180	400	Fairly hot
7	220	200	425	Hot
8	230	210	450	Very hot
9	240	220	475	Very hot

APPROXIMATE WEIGHT CONVERSIONS
• All the recipes in this book list both imperial and metric measurements. Conversions are approximate and have been rounded up or down. Follow one set of measurements only; do not mix the two.
• Cup measurements, which are used by cooks in Australia and America, have not been listed here as they vary from ingredient to ingredient. Please use kitchen scales to measure dry/solid ingredients.

SPOON MEASURES

- Spoon measurements are level unless otherwise specified.
- 1 teaspoon = 5ml
- 1 tablespoon = 15ml
- 1 Australian tablespoon = 20ml (cooks in Australia should measure 3 teaspoons where 1 tablespoon is specified in a recipe)

APPROXIMATE LIQUID CONVERSIONS

metric	imperial	AUS	US
50ml	2fl oz	¼ cup	¼ cup
125ml	4fl oz	½ cup	½ cup
175ml	6fl oz	¾ cup	¾ cup
225ml	8fl oz	1 cup	1 cup
300ml	10fl oz/½ pint	½ pint	1¼ cups
450ml	16fl oz	2 cups	2 cups/1 pint
600ml	20fl oz/1 pint	1 pint	2½ cups
1 litre	35fl oz/1¾ pints	1¾ pints	1 quart

This is a brilliantly easy idea for a starter. And if you're having a barbecue, it's great to snack on while the rest of your food is cooking.

Prawns with Chilli Mayo

400g cooked prawns in shells
2 anchovy fillets from a can or jar
1 fresh red chilli
4 tbsp mayonnaise
1 little gem lettuce
lemon wedges, to serve

Takes 10 minutes • Serves 2

1 Divide the prawns between two glass tumblers. Finely chop the anchovies. Halve and seed the chilli, then finely chop the chilli flesh.
2 Mix the mayonnaise with the anchovies and chilli, and divide between two small dishes.
3 Cut the lettuce into wedges and serve the prawns with the mayo, lettuce and lemon wedges for squeezing over the prawns.

• Per serving 293 kcalories, protein 19g, carbohydrate 1g, fat 24g, saturated fat 4g, fibre 1g, added sugar none, salt 3.69g

Try this as a starter for
a special meal for two.

Scallops with Chilli and Lime

2 tbsp olive oil
10 scallops
2 large garlic cloves, chopped
2 tsp chopped fresh red chilli
juice of 1 lime
small handful of fresh coriander,
roughly chopped

Takes 10–15 minutes • Serves 2

1 Heat the oil in a non-stick frying pan until hot, add the scallops and pan fry for 1 minute until golden underneath. Flip them over and sprinkle with the garlic and chilli.
2 Cook for 1 minute more, then pour over the lime juice and season with salt and pepper. Serve immediately, scattered with the coriander.

• Per serving 260 kcalories, protein 34g, carbohydrate 2g, fat 13g, saturated fat 2g, fibre 0.3g, added sugar none, salt 0.99g

Serve this zingy salad before or after a warming winter
casserole – it's really refreshing.

Chicory and Pear Salad

1 head of red chicory, or white if not
available, trimmed
1 ripe red Williams pear
handful of rocket leaves
small handful of hazelnuts, toasted
and chopped

FOR THE DRESSING
½ tsp green peppercorns in brine
(optional)
1 tbsp hazelnut or olive oil
1 tbsp mild salad oil, such as
sunflower or safflower
½ tsp sherry or cider vinegar

Takes 15–20 minutes • Serves 2

1 Make the dressing. If using green
peppercorns, lightly crush them in a bowl
with a wooden spoon, or use a pestle and
mortar. Mix in the oils and vinegar and add
salt to taste.
2 Carefully separate the chicory leaves and
arrange 5–6 on two plates – if they are big,
cut or tear each one into pieces.
3 Remove the stalk from the pear and
quarter the pear lengthways. Core, then
thinly slice the fruit. Arrange the pear slices
on top of the chicory leaves and spoon over
half the dressing. Pour the remaining
dressing over the rocket and season with salt
and pepper. Give the leaves a quick toss
and pile on top of each salad. Sprinkle with
the nuts and serve.

• Per serving 202 kcalories, protein 2.3g,
carbohydrate 8.9g, fat 17.7g, saturated fat 1.6g,
fibre 3g, added sugar none, salt 0.01g

This starter is incredibly simple – the cooking is minimal and the taste fresh, light and summery.

Roasted Tomato Bruschetta

2 slices of bread from a
close-textured loaf
1 tbsp extra-virgin olive oil
175g/6oz small or cherry vine
tomatoes
2 garlic cloves, peeled
little balsamic vinegar
few fresh basil leaves

Takes 20–25 minutes • Serves 2

1 Preheat the oven to 200°C/Gas 6/fan oven 180°C. Brush the bread on both sides with half the oil. Grill on both sides until toasted.

2 Put the vine tomatoes and garlic in an ovenproof dish in one layer, and drizzle with the remaining oil and some salt and pepper. Bake for 10 minutes until lightly charred and softened. Leave to cool to room temperature.

3 Put a slice of bread on each serving plate. Squash one garlic clove onto each slice and top with the tomatoes along with their cooking juices. Sprinkle each with a few drops of balsamic vinegar and scatter with some roughly torn basil leaves.

• Per serving 207 kcalories, protein 6.2g, carbohydrate 30.1g, fat 7.7g, saturated fat 0.8g, fibre 2.2g, added sugar none, salt 0.7g

Mustard, olive oil and Worcestershire sauce give these mushrooms
a wonderful spicy flavour, creating tasty juices during cooking.

Devilled Mushrooms

1 tbsp wholegrain mustard
1 tbsp olive oil
1 tbsp Worcestershire sauce
1 garlic clove, crushed
4 large flat mushrooms
½ tsp paprika
½ × 140g bag mixed salad leaves,
with ruby chard and watercress
French or crusty bread, to serve

Takes about 20 minutes • Serves 2

1 Preheat the oven to 200°C/Gas 6/fan oven 180°C. In a large bowl, mix together the mustard, oil, Worcestershire sauce and garlic, then season with salt and freshly ground black pepper.
2 Add the mushrooms to the mixture and toss well to coat them evenly. (You can do this ahead and let them marinate while you prepare the rest of the meal.) Place them stalk-side up in a roasting tin and sprinkle over the paprika. Bake for 8–10 minutes.
3 Divide the salad leaves between two serving plates. Put two mushrooms on each plate and spoon over the juices. Serve straight away, with French or crusty bread.

• Per serving 102 kcalories, protein 5g, carbohydrate 3.7g, fat 7.6g, saturated fat 1g, fibre 3g, added sugar 0.3g, salt 0.57g

This salad has really Christmassy flavours and is a lovely light alternative to heavy festive meals.

Cheese and Cranberry Salad

100g goat's cheese (round with a rind)
1 ripe pear
oil, for brushing
handful of pecan nuts, roughly broken
80g bag mixed watercress and spinach
crusty bread, to serve

FOR THE DRESSING
1 tbsp cranberry sauce
1 tbsp olive oil
1 tbsp lemon juice

Takes 20–30 minutes • Serves 2

1 Preheat the grill to high and line the grill rack with foil. Halve the cheese to make two discs. Halve and core the pear, cut each half into slices and arrange in two piles on the foil. Lightly brush the pears with oil then top each pile with a cheese disc (cut side up) and grill for a few minutes until lightly golden and bubbling. Scatter with the nuts and grill for a minute or so more.

2 For the dressing, whisk the cranberry sauce with the oil and lemon juice and season.

3 Arrange salad leaves on two plates. Put the pears and cheese on top. Spoon over the dressing, scatter over any stray nuts and eat straight away with crusty bread while the cheese is still deliciously runny.

• Per serving 327 kcalories, protein 13g, carbohydrate 12g, fat 26g, saturated fat 10g, fibre 3g, added sugar 2g, salt 0.99g

A fantastic way to use up leftovers.
For extra crunch, add some baby corn or beansprouts.

Warm Chicken Noodle Salad

50g or 1 bundle of rice noodles
(such as Thai stir-fry noodles)
100g/4oz sugar snaps, halved
lengthways
1 small red pepper, seeded and
thinly sliced
handful of fresh basil
2 cooked boneless, skinless chicken
breasts

FOR THE DRESSING
3 tbsp olive oil
finely grated zest and juice
of ½ lemon
1 heaped tbsp mayonnaise

Takes 15–20 minutes • Serves 2

1 Boil the kettle and tip the rice noodles into a heatproof bowl. Pour over boiling water to cover. Leave the noodles to soak for 4 minutes.
2 Meanwhile, make the dressing. Whisk together the olive oil, lemon zest and juice and mayonnaise, then season to taste. Drain the noodles and return to the bowl. Throw in the sugar snaps, red pepper and basil. Pour in half the dressing and gently toss.
3 Divide the noodles between two bowls. Slice the chicken breasts and arrange on top of the noodles. Drizzle over the remaining dressing and serve.

• Per serving 577 kcalories, protein 40g, carbohydrate 28g, fat 35g, saturated fat 6g, fibre 2g, added sugar none, salt 0.40g

An unusual and superhealthy salad that will make
a weekday meal a little bit special.

Lamb and Orange Salad

2 × 140g/5oz lamb leg steaks,
trimmed of all fat
2 small oranges (blood oranges are
good when in season)
1 carrot, coarsely grated
2 large handfuls winter salad leaves
small bunch fresh flatleaf parsley,
leaves only

FOR THE DRESSING
1 tbsp olive oil
1 tsp balsamic or sherry vinegar
1 small garlic clove, crushed

Takes 15 minutes • Serves 2

1 Heat a cast iron ridged griddle pan until very hot. Rub the lamb steaks with a drop of oil, season, then cook for 5 minutes, turning once, for a medium steak. Cover with foil and set aside to rest.

2 Cut away the skin and pith of the oranges and thinly slice. Drain off the excess juices.

3 Whisk together the dressing ingredients and season to taste. Drain any meat and orange juices into the dressing, then toss with the carrot, oranges, salad leaves and parsley.

4 Slice the lamb and serve on top of the salad.

• Per serving 346 kcalories, protein 32g, carbohydrate 15g, fat 18g, saturated fat 5g, fibre 115g, added sugar none, salt 0.57g

This is a bistro-style salad, using smoked haddock
instead of the more usual bacon.

Smoked Haddock Salad

1 tbsp wholegrain mustard
1 tbsp cider or white wine vinegar,
plus an extra splash
5 tbsp olive oil
½ small loaf of French bread,
torn into bite-size pieces
180g pack trimmed French beans
300g/10oz skinned smoked haddock
2 eggs
half a head of frisée, split into leaves

Takes 25–30 minutes • Serves 2

1 For the dressing whisk the mustard, vinegar, 3 tablespoons of oil, 1 tablespoon of water and a pinch of salt. Scatter the bread on a baking sheet, drizzle with the remaining oil and toast under a preheated grill for 8–10 minutes.
2 Meanwhile, boil the beans for 3–5 minutes until still slightly crunchy. Remove with a slotted spoon and toss in some of the dressing. Lower the heat, add the haddock and gently poach for 5 minutes. Transfer to a plate, add a splash of vinegar to the water, break in the eggs and poach for 3 minutes. Remove and drain.
3 Tip the frisée leaves into a large bowl and flake the haddock over in big chunks. Toss in the bread, beans and most of the dressing. Serve warm, topped with the eggs and drizzled with the remaining dressing.

• Per serving 627 kcalories, protein 43g, carbohydrate 32g, fat 37g, saturated fat 6g, fibre 4g, added sugar none, salt 4.2g

There's no need to cook the couscous –
just soak it and mix in the tasty bits.

Mediterranean Couscous Salad

100g/4oz couscous
200ml/7fl oz hot vegetable stock
5 sun-dried or sunblush tomatoes,
quartered
1 medium avocado, peeled, stoned
and cut into large chunks
50g/2oz black olives
handful of nuts, such as pine nuts,
cashews or almonds
100g/4oz feta, roughly crumbled
½ × 130g bag green salad leaves

FOR THE DRESSING
2½ tbsp olive oil
1 tbsp lemon juice

Takes 10–20 minutes • Serves 2

1 Tip the couscous into a large bowl, stir
in the hot stock, cover and leave to soak
for 5 minutes.
2 Make a dressing with the olive oil, lemon juice
and some salt and pepper. Stir 1 tablespoon
into the couscous, then gently mix in the
tomatoes, avocado, olives, nuts and feta.
Taste for seasoning.
3 Toss the salad leaves with the remaining
dressing, divide between two plates and
spoon the couscous on top.

• Per serving 608 kcalories, protein 16g, carbohydrate
33g, fat 46.6g, saturated fat 11g, fibre 4.4g, added
sugar none, salt 4.79g

Swap the mozzarella for blue cheese and the basil for chives
for a totally different taste.

Warm Mediterranean New Potato Salad

1 tbsp olive oil
2 garlic cloves
500g bag baby new potatoes
500ml/18fl oz vegetable stock
125g ball mozzarella, torn into
bite-sized pieces
500g pack cherry tomatoes, halved
50g/2oz pine nuts, toasted
handful of fresh basil leaves, sliced

Takes 30 minutes • Serves 2

1 Heat the oil in a large frying pan and fry the garlic and potatoes for 1–2 minutes. Pour over the stock and simmer, uncovered, for 20 minutes or until the potatoes are cooked. Turn the heat up and let the stock reduce to about 2 tablespoons of sticky glaze.

2 Throw in the mozzarella, tomatoes, pine nuts and basil and give it a stir. When the cheese starts to melt, remove the pan from the heat and share between two plates. Serve with crisp lettuce leaves on the side.

• Per serving 615 kcalories, protein 23g, carbohydrate 50g, fat 37g, saturated fat 11g, fibre 6g, added sugar none, salt 1.6g

When you need an emergency meal in a hurry,
nothing beats this tasty snack to share.

Speedy Nachos

175g pack plain tortilla chips
225g jar salsa
2–3 spring onions, sliced
50–85g/2–3oz fontina or cheddar cheese
pinch of crushed dried chilli flakes
soured cream or guacamole, to serve (optional)

Takes 5–10 minutes •
Serves 2 generously

1 Preheat the grill to high. Tip the tortilla chips onto a baking sheet and pour the salsa over. Scatter over the spring onions.
2 Grate the cheese over, and sprinkle with the chilli flakes.
3 Grill for about 3 minutes to melt the cheese. Serve with soured cream or guacamole, if you like.

• Per serving (without soured cream or guacamole) 560 kcalories, protein 16g, carbohydrate 62.6g, fat 29.1g, saturated fat 5.5g, fibre 6.2g, added sugar 1.1g, salt 5.26g

Whizz up this easy storecupboard dip and
you have the perfect lunch for two.

Red Pepper Houmous

410g can chickpeas
1 large garlic clove
2 roasted red peppers from a jar
1 tbsp lemon juice
2 tbsp olive oil, plus a little extra for
drizzling
½ tsp chilli powder
celery sticks and radishes with the
leaves on, and Italian breadsticks,
to serve

Takes 5–10 minutes •
Serves 2 generously

1 Rinse and drain the chickpeas, then tip them into a food processor. Peel the garlic and crush in with the chickpeas, along with plenty of salt and pepper. Whizz briefly.
2 Remove any stray seeds from the peppers, then add the peppers to the processor with the lemon juice, olive oil and chilli. Blitz again until really smooth. Taste and add extra seasoning and chilli for more of a kick, if you like.
3 Spoon into a bowl, drizzle with olive oil and serve with celery sticks, radishes and a stack of breadsticks for dipping.

• Per serving 407 kcalories, protein 11g, carbohydrate 27g, fat 29g, saturated fat 3g, fibre 7g, added sugar none, salt 2.23g

This snack is not the healthiest option, but it's meltingly good and a great treat when you want to eat quickly.

Pan-fried Camembert Sandwich

butter, for spreading
4 thick slices of white bread, from
a rustic loaf is good
175g/6oz camembert
2 spoonfuls of cranberry sauce
balsamic vinegar, for drizzling
(optional)

Takes 5–10 minutes • Serves 2

1 Butter the slices of bread. Cut the camembert into 2 wedges. Lay each wedge on the unbuttered sides of two slices of the bread.
2 Top with a spoonful of cranberry sauce. Drizzle with a few drops of balsamic vinegar, if using. Put the two other slices of bread on top of each, buttered sides on the outside.
3 Fry in a hot non-stick pan for a minute or two on each side, pressing down with a fish slice to flatten, until golden brown and melting. Cut each sandwich in half and eat straight away.

• Per serving 547 kcalories, protein 26.3g, carbohydrate 46.4g, fat 29.8g, saturated fat 18.7g, fibre 1.3g, added sugar 1.7g, salt 2.66g

Goat's cheese is great for grilling – it browns nicely without toughening. For those with big appetites, you can simply double the quantities.

Posh Cheese on Toast

1 small ciabatta (about 175g/6oz), split in half, or 2 thick slices of sourdough bread
50g/2oz marinated peppers or 2 heaped tbsp tomato or onion relish
8 pitted black olives, sliced
100g/4oz semi-soft goat's cheese, such as chèvre
2 tsp aged balsamic vinegar (optional)
few leaves of watercress or rocket
extra-virgin olive oil

Takes 12–15 minutes • Serves 2

1 Heat the grill to medium. Toast the bread, lightly, on the rounded side. Spread the other, flat side with the peppers or relish and scatter over the olives.
2 Crumble over the cheese and return to the grill until the cheese softens and starts to brown.
3 Remove from the grill and drizzle with the balsamic vinegar, if using. Serve, topped with a small handful of watercress or rocket and a drizzle of olive oil over the top, while the cheese is still hot and bubbling.

• Per serving 485 kcalories, protein 20g, carbohydrate 48g, fat 25g, saturated fat 10g, fibre 3g, added sugar none, salt 3.48g

Instead of caramelised onions, try a few roasted peppers from a jar.

Steak and Caramelised Onion Sandwich

4 minute steaks or 2 × 1cm thick sirloin steaks
olive oil, for frying and drizzling
1 small ciabatta loaf
4 tbsp caramelised onions from a jar
½ × 85g bag watercress

Takes 10–15 minutes •
Serves 2 generously

1 Heat the grill to medium. Heat a little oil in a frying pan. Season both sides of the steaks with salt, then fry for 1–2 minutes on each side. Meanwhile, slice the ciabatta in half lengthways and grill the cut sides until golden.

2 Drizzle the toasted ciabatta with olive oil, spread the bottom half with the onions and sit the steaks on top.

3 Cover with the watercress and close the sandwich with the other half of the ciabatta. Cut into four sandwiches and serve two per person. Serve hot.

• Per serving 525 kcalories, protein 52g, carbohydrate 33g, fat 21g, saturated fat 5g, fibre 2g, added sugar 2g, salt 1.85g

For a spicy hit, sprinkle the turkey with
Cajun seasoning before grilling.

Open Turkey BLT

2 turkey steaks, about 140g/5oz
each
4 rashers smoked streaky bacon
2 slices melting cheese, such as
cheddar or Gruyère
half a loaf of ciabatta, cut in half
horizontally
2 tbsp mayonnaise
1 medium tomato, sliced
½ avocado, peeled, stoned and
thinly sliced
4 lettuce leaves (little gem is good)

Takes 15–20 minutes • Serves 2

1 Heat the grill to high. Lay the turkey steaks
and bacon on a large baking tray and grill for
3 minutes on each side or until cooked
through. Set the bacon aside and top the
turkey steaks with the cheese slices.
2 Put the ciabatta slices next to the turkey in
the pan and return them both to the grill until
the bread is toasted and the cheese is
melted.
3 Spread the toast with the mayonnaise and
top with the cheesy turkey steaks, tomato,
avocado, lettuce and bacon.

• Per serving 685 kcalories, protein 54g, carbohydrate
42g, fat 35g, saturated fat 9g, fibre 3g, added sugar
none, salt 3g

If you're a keen meat eater, use leftover chicken or lamb instead of cheese – just warm through with the peppers.

Roasted Pepper and Halloumi Wraps

2 thick slices halloumi cheese
½ tsp dried oregano
1 tbsp olive oil
2 Arab flat breads (they look like circular pitta bread)
2 roasted red peppers from a jar
6 slices roasted aubergine from a jar
handful kalamata olives
2–4 lemon wedges
good handful fresh flatleaf parsley sprigs

Takes 10 minutes • Serves 2

1 Sprinkle both sides of the halloumi with the oregano. Heat the oil in a non-stick frying pan, then briefly fry the halloumi on both sides until golden. Remove from the pan, but leave the pan on the heat. Heat the flat breads over a naked gas flame for a few seconds on each side to warm them. (Alternatively you can do this in a large frying pan.)
2 Halve the peppers (removing any stray seeds) and thickly slice, then add to the pan with the aubergine, olives and fried halloumi. Heat through, squeeze over two of the lemon wedges and season well. To serve, divide the mixture and the parsley sprigs between the wraps, and top each with a lemon wedge for squeezing over, if you like.

• Per serving 561 kcalories, protein 14g, carbohydrate 51g, fat 35g, saturated fat 8g, fibre 5g, added sugar none, salt 0.91g

A good midweek snack
that's ready in a jiffy.

Storecupboard Rarebit

2 thick slices of wholemeal bread
85g/3oz mature cheddar, grated
½ small red onion, finely chopped
2 small tomatoes, roughly chopped
1 medium egg
pinch of cayenne pepper (optional)

Takes 15–20 minutes • Serves 2

1 Heat the grill to medium and toast the bread on both sides. Set the toast aside, but keep the grill on.

2 In a bowl combine the cheese, onion, tomatoes, egg and cayenne, if using. Give it all a good stir and season well with salt and pepper. Divide the cheesy mix between the two slices of toast and spread it out so it completely covers the toast.

3 Slide the toast back under the grill and cook until golden brown and bubbling. Eat while it's hot.

• Per serving 315 kcalories, protein 18g, carbohydrate 20g, fat 16g, saturated fat 10g, fibre 3g, added sugar none, salt 1.39g

For a vegetarian version, stir fry chunks of tofu instead of prawns, or add extra veg such as water chestnuts or shredded pak choi.

Scrambled Egg Stir Fry

1 tbsp oil
100g/4oz cooked prawns, defrosted and patted dry if frozen
thumb-sized knob of ginger, washed and grated (no need to peel)
large handful of fresh beansprouts
4 spring onions, sliced
4 eggs, beaten
1 tbsp soy sauce, plus extra to taste

Takes 10 minutes • Serves 2

1 Heat the oil in a wok or frying pan and stir fry the prawns on a high heat for 20 seconds until they start to take on a little colour.
2 Tip in the ginger, beansprouts and half of the spring onions and stir fry for another 30 seconds, then turn down the heat and pour in the eggs.
3 Leave to set for a few seconds, then move the loosely set egg around the pan with a spatula to scramble. When all of the egg has set, tip in the soy sauce and let it sizzle for a few seconds. Serve sprinkled with the rest of the spring onion and season with more soy sauce to taste.

• Per serving 296 kcalories, protein 28g, carbohydrate 2g, fat 20g, saturated fat 4g, fibre 1g, added sugar 0.1g, salt 3.81g

Try this delicious cheesy scramble
for a late-breakfast treat for two.

Cheese and Watercress Scramble

2 soda farls (usually sold in packs
of 2, alongside bread and rolls)
4 large eggs
4 tbsp milk
50g/2oz mature cheddar cheese
generous knob of butter, plus extra
for spreading
10 cherry tomatoes
generous handful of watercress

Takes 10 minutes • Serves 2

1 Split the soda farls and toast on both sides. Meanwhile, beat together the eggs and milk with some salt and black pepper. Grate the cheese. Butter the farls and put on serving plates.

2 Melt the butter in a small-to-medium-sized frying pan (preferably non-stick) then add the tomatoes and cook them for about 3 minutes over a fairly high heat, shaking the pan occasionally until they start to soften and the skins split.

3 Pour the eggs into the pan and leave them undisturbed for about 10 seconds. Stir and leave to settle again, then stir again until the eggs are almost scrambled. Sprinkle in the cheese, roughly chop and add the watercress, then remove from the heat. Pile the scramble on top of the farls and serve straight away.

• Per serving 765 kcalories, protein 32g, carbohydrate 36g, fat 56g, saturated fat 22g, fibre 2g, added sugar none, salt 1.57g

A creative way of using Italian ingredients that's speedy
and easy too – perfect for people on the go.

Mozzarella, Ham and Pesto Pizzas

4 mini pitta breads
150g pack mozzarella
4 tsp pesto
85g/3oz smoked wafer-thin ham

Takes 10 minutes • Serves 2

1 Heat the grill to high, put the pittas on the grill rack and heat for about 1 minute while you slice the mozzarella into 5.

2 Turn the pittas over and spread each one with 1 teaspoon pesto, then top with a mozzarella slice. Pile the ham on top, so it looks quite ruffled, then tear the final mozzarella slice into 4, put it on top of the ham and grind over some black pepper.

3 Return to the grill for 3–4 minutes more until melted and starting to turn golden.

• Per serving 491 kcalories, protein 36g, carbohydrate 41g, fat 21g, saturated fat 12g, fibre 1.6g, added sugar none, salt 3.34g

A New York deli snack for two
that microwaves in minutes.

Hot Pastrami Bagels

2 onion bagels
butter, for spreading
American mustard
120g pack pastrami (cured beef brisket)
2 dill pickles
handful of torn iceberg lettuce leaves

Takes 15 minutes • Serves 2

1 Split the bagels and spread each of the cut sides with butter and a little mustard. Separate the slices of pastrami, sandwich them between the bagels and put them on a sheet of double-thickness kitchen paper on a microwave-proof plate – the paper stops the bread from becoming soggy underneath and sticking to the plate. Microwave on medium for 1 minute.

2 While the bagels are warming, slice the dill pickles lengthways.

3 Take the bagels from the microwave and lift off their tops. Pile in the lettuce and sliced pickles, squirt in some more mustard and enjoy straight away while they're still warm.

• Per serving 241 kcalories, protein 17g, carbohydrate 27g, fat 8g, saturated fat 3g, fibre 2g, added sugar none, salt 3.04g

Try using small chunks of unpeeled potato
instead of the polenta.

Crispy Italian Chicken and Polenta

500g pack ready-to-use polenta
25g/1oz parmesan, grated
2 boneless chicken breasts, skin on
250g pack cherry tomatoes
leaves from a few fresh rosemary
sprigs, torn
1 garlic clove, sliced
2 tbsp olive oil

Takes 30 minutes • Serves 2

1 Preheat the oven to 220°C/Gas 7/fan oven 200°C. Using your fingers, roughly break up the polenta into small chunks and scatter over the bottom of a small roasting tin. Tip in the parmesan and mix.

2 Sit the chicken breasts, cherry tomatoes, rosemary and garlic on top of the polenta, drizzle with olive oil, then season to taste.

3 Roast for 25 minutes or until the chicken skin is crisp and golden, and the polenta and cheese are turning crusty around the edges. Serve with a green salad.

• Per serving 513 kcalories, protein 40g, carbohydrate 47g, fat 20g, saturated fat 5g, fibre 7g, added sugar none, salt 4.63g

If you want a meal for two in a hurry, try this filling and tasty dish. Don't worry about precise measures – just add as much as you want.

Curried Chicken with Cashew Rice

1 tbsp curry paste
1 fresh red or green chilli, chopped (optional)
250g packet cooked basmati rice
about 100g/4oz cooked chicken, shredded
handful of frozen peas
50g packet roasted cashews
squeeze of fresh lemon juice

Takes 10 minutes • Serves 2

1 Spoon the curry paste into a wok or large frying pan and heat it up. If you like spicy food, add the chilli.
2 Stir in the rice, chicken, peas and cashews.
3 Stir fry until piping hot, then season with a squeeze of lemon juice.

• Per serving 428 kcalories, protein 24g, carbohydrate 43g, fat 19g, saturated fat 1g, fibre 2g, added sugar 1g, salt 1.18g

Tenderstem broccoli is ideal for this dish as it cooks so quickly. Add a couple of minutes to the cooking time if you're using ordinary broccoli.

Broccoli Lemon Chicken

1 tbsp groundnut or sunflower oil
340g pack of mini chicken breast fillets (sometimes called goujons)
2 garlic cloves, sliced
200g pack tenderstem broccoli, stems halved if very long
200ml/7fl oz chicken stock
1 heaped tsp cornflour
1 tbsp clear honey or 2 tsp golden caster sugar
zest and juice of 1 lemon
large handful of roasted cashews
basmati rice or noodles, to serve

Takes 15–25 minutes • Serves 2

1 Heat the oil in a large frying pan or wok. Add the chicken and fry for 3–4 minutes until golden. Remove from the pan and add the garlic and broccoli. Stir fry for a minute or so then cover and cook for 2 minutes more, until almost tender.

2 Mix the stock, cornflour and honey or sugar well, then pour into the pan and stir until thickened.

3 Tip the chicken back into the pan and let it heat through, then add the lemon zest and juice, and cashew nuts. Stir, then serve straight away with basmati rice or noodles.

• Per serving 372 kcalories, protein 48g, carbohydrate 15g, fat 13g, saturated fat 2g, fibre 3g, added sugar 6g, salt 0.69g

A simple idea for turning chicken breasts into something special – it's so tasty you'll want to eat it again and again!

Honey Glazed Chicken

2 boneless chicken breasts, skin on
½ lemon
1 tbsp clear honey
1 tbsp dark soy sauce

TO SERVE
green salad and potatoes roasted with herbs and garlic

Takes 40 minutes • Serves 2

1 Preheat the oven to 190°C/Gas 5/fan oven 170°C. Lay the chicken, skin-side up, in a small baking or roasting dish. Season.
2 Squeeze the lemon juice into a bowl and stir in the honey and soy sauce. Spoon this mixture over the chicken, then tuck the squeezed-out half of the lemon between the pieces (to moisten and add flavour).
3 Roast, uncovered, for 30–35 minutes until done and richly glazed, basting with the juices at least twice. Serve with a salad and roasted potatoes.

• Per serving 197 kcalories, protein 32.4g, carbohydrate 8.6g, fat 3.9g, saturated fat 1.3g, fibre 0.3g, added sugar 6g, salt 1.91g

A fresh and delicious dish
that's good enough to eat every day.

Saucy Chicken and Spring Vegetables

2 boneless chicken breasts, skin on
1 tbsp olive oil
200g/8oz baby new potatoes, thinly
sliced
500ml/18fl oz chicken stock
200g pack mixed spring vegetables
(broccoli, peas, broad beans and
sliced courgette)
2 tbsp crème fraîche
handful of fresh tarragon leaves,
roughly chopped

Takes 25–30 minutes • Serves 2

1 Fry the chicken in the oil in a wok or large frying pan for 5 minutes on each side. Throw in the potatoes and stir to coat. Pour the chicken stock over, cover and simmer for 10 minutes until the potatoes are almost cooked through.

2 Remove the lid and turn the heat to high. Reduce the stock until it just coats the bottom of the pan and there's enough left to cook the vegetables. Scatter the vegetables into the pan, cover again and cook the veg for about 2 minutes.

3 Stir in the crème fraîche to make a creamy sauce, season with salt and pepper, if you like, then add the tarragon. Serve straight from the pan.

• Per serving 386 kcalories, protein 38g, carbohydrate 23g, fat 16g, saturated fat 6g, fibre 3g, added sugar none, salt 1.5g

This revival of an old family-favourite is updated as a stylish dish for two with a Thai-style pineapple salsa.

Gammon with Pineapple Salsa

1 large gammon steak, rind on, about 350g/12oz (1cm/½in thick)
a little oil, for brushing
1 tsp clear honey

FOR THE SALSA
100g/4oz fresh pineapple, finely chopped
1 large fresh red chilli, seeded and finely chopped
1 tsp light muscovado sugar
1 tsp soy sauce
1 tbsp chopped fresh coriander

Takes 20 minutes • Serves 2

1 First, make the salsa. Mix together all of the ingredients (use ½ a chilli for a milder flavour, all of it for a pungent one). Set aside while you cook the gammon.
2 Preheat the grill to high for 3 minutes. Use a thin-bladed knife to slice the gammon into 2 steaks, then snip the rind every 2–3cm/¾–1¼ in. Lightly brush with oil. Grill for about 3 minutes on each side until just firm, then brush over the honey on one side and cook for 1 minute more. Remove and leave to stand for 2–3 minutes.
3 Serve the gammon with the salsa spooned over the top. This is good with a chicory salad or green beans and chunky-cut chips.

• Per serving 283 kcalories, protein 32g, carbohydrate 10g, fat 13g, saturated fat 4g, fibre 1g, added sugar 5g, salt 6.12g

Try swapping the pork chops
for chicken breasts for a delicious variation.

Mustardy Pork Chops

2 pork chops
1 tsp wholegrain mustard
25g/1oz cheddar, grated
2 tsp crème fraîche or cream

Takes 25 minutes • Serves 2

1 Preheat the oven to 200°C/Gas 6/fan oven 180°C. Place the chops in a large, shallow roasting tray and bake for 15 minutes.
2 Mix together the mustard, cheddar and crème fraîche or cream. Spread over the top of the chops.
3 Return to the oven for 5 minutes until the cheese is melting and bubbling. Serve with some potato wedges (which can be cooked in the oven at the same time as the chops) and seasonal green vegetables.

• Per serving 435 kcalories, protein 44.1g, carbohydrate 0.2g, fat 28.6g, saturated fat 12.5g, fibre 0.1g, added sugar none, salt 0.58g

When you're feeling a bit disheartened by the long winter evenings,
try this warming one-bowl wonder.

Speedy Chorizo with Chickpeas

400g can chopped tomatoes
110g pack chorizo (unsliced)
140g/5oz wedge Savoy cabbage
sprinkling of dried chilli flakes
410g can chickpeas, drained
1 chicken or vegetable stock cube

Takes 10 minutes • Serves 2

1 Put a medium pan on the heat and tip in the tomatoes followed by a canful of water. While the tomatoes are heating, quickly chop the chorizo into chunky pieces and shred the cabbage.

2 Pile the chorizo and cabbage into the pan with the chilli flakes and chickpeas, then crumble in the stock cube.

3 Stir well, cover and leave to bubble over a high heat for 6 minutes until the cabbage is just tender. Ladle into two bowls and eat with crusty or garlic bread.

• Per serving 366 kcalories, protein 23g, carbohydrate 30g, fat 18g, saturated fat 5g, fibre 9g, added sugar 0.3g, salt 4.26g

If you want a lighter version, use half-fat crème fraîche and 50g/2oz of parmesan instead of the gruyère.

Purple Sprouting Broccoli Grill

500g/1lb purple sprouting broccoli, about 18 stems
200ml carton crème fraîche
1 tbsp wholegrain mustard
100g/4oz grated cheese, such as gruyère or cheddar
6 slices ham

Takes 20 minutes • Serves 2

1 Bring a pan of water to the boil, add the broccoli and blanch for 2 minutes. Drain into a colander and refresh under running cold water.

2 In a small bowl, mix the crème fraîche with the mustard and half the cheese. Preheat the grill to high.

3 Use each slice of ham to wrap up three stems of broccoli then place in a baking dish in a higgledy-piggledy fashion. Spread the creamy mixture over, sprinkle with the remaining cheese and grill for 10 minutes until golden and bubbly.

• Per serving 755 kcalories, protein 39g, carbohydrate 10g, fat 62g, saturated fat 38g, fibre 9g, added sugars none, salt 3.38g

When the weather's good, try cooking these on the barbecue. The lamb will be juicy and tender – a wonderful summer treat.

Sizzled Lamb with Chilli Tomatoes

140g/5oz ripe vine tomatoes
½ small red onion
½ fresh red chilli
1 tbsp chopped fresh coriander
2 lamb leg steaks
olive oil

Takes 20 minutes • Serves 2

1 Halve the tomatoes, then squeeze out and discard the seeds. Finely chop the tomato flesh and onion. Halve, seed and finely chop the chilli. Mix the tomatoes, onion and chilli in a bowl with the coriander and some salt and pepper. At this point the tomato mixture can be covered and chilled for up to 2 days, but bring it back to room temperature before serving.

2 Season the lamb steaks on both sides and rub with a little olive oil.

3 Barbecue or cook on a hot griddle pan for 3–4 minutes each side for medium, a little longer if you prefer your lamb well done. Serve each leg steak with a dollop of the chilli tomatoes, new potatoes and a big crunchy salad.

• Per serving 293 kcalories, protein 34.7g, carbohydrate 3.5g, fat 15.7g, saturated fat 7.3g, fibre 0.9g, added sugar none, salt 0.49g

Look for stir-fry sauces and
no-need-to-cook noodles in the supermarket.

Steak and Noodle Stir Fry

225g/8oz rump steak
225g/8oz pak choi (Chinese greens)
1 red pepper, seeded
2 tbsp sunflower oil
100–120g sachet stir fry sauce
2 × 150g packs no-cook noodles

Takes 10 minutes • Serves 2

1 Trim any visible fat from the steak, then slice into thin strips. Cut each head of pak choi into four lengthways. Dice the pepper into small squares.

2 Heat two tablespoons of sunflower oil in a pan. Add the pepper and fry quickly for 1 minute. Add the beef and fry until browned all over. Add the pak choi and cook briefly until starting to wilt.

3 Tip in the stir fry sauce and 2 tablespoons of water and stir. Bring to the boil, then add the noodles and warm through, loosening them until they are all coated in sauce. Serve immediately.

• Per serving 499 kcalories, protein 32g, carbohydrate 53.8g, fat 18.9g, saturated fat 3.1g, fibre 3.8g, added sugar 1.6g, salt 2.52g

A really versatile recipe – try chopped red pepper instead of the bacon.

Spaghetti with 5-minute Tomato Sauce

5 large ripe tomatoes
140g/5oz spaghetti
3 tbsp olive oil
100g/4oz diced bacon or lardons
2 garlic cloves, chopped
50–85g/2–3oz soft fresh rindless goat's cheese
handful of fresh basil and/or snipped chives

Takes 20–25 minutes • Serves 2

1 Pour boiling water over the tomatoes to cover, leave for 1 minute, then drain and remove the skins. Quarter and seed the tomatoes, chop the flesh.
2 Bring a large pan of salted water to the boil, add the spaghetti and stir. Cook according to packet instructions. Meanwhile, heat 1 tablespoon of the oil in a frying pan, add the bacon and fry until starting to crisp up. Add the garlic, tomatoes, the rest of the oil and salt and pepper, if liked. Heat through for 1–2 minutes until just simmering.
3 Drain the spaghetti and add to the pan, tossing in the sauce until lightly coated. Divide between two warm soup plates, crumble over the cheese and scatter over the herbs. Serve with crusty bread and a glass of red wine.

• Per serving 637 kcalories, protein 23g, carbohydrate 63g, fat 35g, saturated fat 10g, fibre 5g, added sugar none, salt 1.98g

Stuffed pasta comes in a wide variety of fillings – choose your favourite for this fantastically quick and tasty recipe.

10-minute Tortellini

250g pack fresh spinach and ricotta tortellini
1 tbsp olive oil
250g pack cherry tomatoes
2 × 20g packs fresh flatleaf parsley leaves, roughly chopped
3 tbsp finely grated parmesan cheese

Takes 5–10 minutes • Serves 2

1 Boil the pasta for 2 minutes until just cooked. Meanwhile, heat the oil in a frying pan and sizzle the tomatoes until they start to blister.

2 When the pasta is cooked, drain it quickly, reserving some cooking water. Put the tomatoes back on a high heat.

3 Tip in the pasta, parsley, a splash of cooking water and most of the parmesan. Bubble everything together and season with salt and pepper, if liked. Serve with the remaining parmesan.

• Per serving 482 kcalories, protein 18g, carbohydrate 62g, fat 20g, saturated fat 8g, fibre 4g, added sugar none, salt 1.5g

This is a delicious and rather special supper for two.
For a cheaper version replace the asparagus with courgette sticks.

Asparagus and Salmon Supper

2 salmon fillets, about 140g/5oz each
100g pack asparagus spears
3 tbsp olive oil
juice of ½ lemon
2 tsp wholegrain mustard
410g can cannellini beans, drained and rinsed
2 large handfuls of baby spinach leaves

Takes 15–20 minutes • Serves 2

1 Put a steamer on to boil. Lay the salmon fillets in the steamer and steam for 3 minutes until the salmon has changed colour. Throw the asparagus spears in with the salmon and continue to steam for 4–5 minutes until the asparagus is tender and the fish is cooked.
2 While everything's steaming, make a dressing by whisking together the olive oil, lemon juice and mustard. Tip the cannellini beans and spinach into a large bowl.
3 When the asparagus is cooked scoop it into the bowl, then stir in the dressing. Sit the salmon on top of the vegetables to serve.

• Per serving 565 kcalories, protein 41g, carbohydrate 25g, fat 32g, saturated fat 5g, fibre 9g, added sugar none, salt 2g

You can cook the parcels in the microwave – cook each one separately for 3 minutes on High, then leave to stand for 2 minutes.

Herby Salmon and Couscous Parcels

110g pack lemon and garlic couscous
200ml/7fl oz hot vegetable stock
1 tbsp olive oil
handful of chopped fresh herbs (parsley, plus thyme, tarragon or rosemary is good)
4 spring onions, thinly sliced
4 sunblush or sun-dried tomatoes, chopped
2 salmon fillets, about 140g/5oz each

Takes 25 minutes • Serves 2

1 Put the couscous into a bowl and stir in the stock and oil. Cover with cling film and leave to stand for 10 minutes, then uncover and fluff up with a fork. Keeping back some herbs, add the rest to the couscous with the spring onions and tomatoes. Season to taste.
2 Preheat the oven to 200°C/Gas 6/fan oven 180°C. Cut out two large sheets of non-stick baking paper, then divide the couscous between them. Sit each fillet on the couscous, top with the remaining herbs and season.
3 Fold the paper over, then twist the edges to seal – like a Cornish pasty. Put the parcels onto a baking sheet and bake for 15 minutes or until the fish feels firm through the paper. Serve in the bag.

• Per serving 504 kcalories, protein 36g, carbohydrate 39g, fat 24g, saturated fat 5g, fibre 1g, added sugar 5g, salt 2.71g

Try the chunky salsa with griddled
chicken breasts or steak.

Griddled Fish with Avocado Salsa

1 ripe avocado
2 ripe plum tomatoes, each
chopped into 6
1 small red onion, finely sliced
3 tbsp olive oil, plus some for
drizzling
juice of ½ lemon or 1 lime
small bunch of fresh coriander,
leaves only
2 × 140g/5oz fish fillets, such as
Pacific cod or halibut, skin on

Takes 15 minutes • Serves 2

1 Halve and stone the avocado and use
a teaspoon to scoop chunks of the flesh into
a bowl. Gently mix all the other ingredients,
except the fish, in with the avocado, then
set aside.
2 Heat a cast iron ridged griddle pan until
very hot. Season the fish with pepper, and
salt if liked, then drizzle with a little olive oil.
3 Griddle the fillets for 2–3 minutes on each
side until charred and cooked through. Serve
with the avocado salsa.

• Per serving 423 kcalories, protein 28g, carbohydrate
6g, fat 32g, saturated fat 4g, fibre 3g, added sugar
none, salt 0.25g

A brilliant way of used canned tuna –
you'll create a fabulous meal for two in just 10 minutes.

Tuna and Feta Frittata

4 large eggs
4 salad onions, sliced diagonally
85g/3oz feta, roughly crumbled
100g can tuna, drained and flaked
1 tbsp olive oil
green leafed salad, to serve

Takes 10 minutes • Serves 2

1 Beat the eggs in a bowl, then stir in the sliced salad onions, feta and flaked tuna. Season with salt (you shouldn't need much as the feta is salty) and pepper.
2 Heat the oil in a medium non-stick pan. Pour the mixture in, then cook, undisturbed, over a low heat for 5 minutes until almost set.
3 Put the pan under a preheated grill for 3–4 minutes, until the frittata is set and golden. Serve in wedges with a salad.

• Per serving 607 kcalories, protein 35.8g, carbohydrate 1.2g, fat 51g, saturated fat 16.5g, fibre 0.2g, added sugar none, salt 2.16g

Pick up the ingredients for this speedy supper on your way home from work, throw them into the wok, then serve with instant egg noodles.

Stir-fry Prawns with Spinach

3 tbsp groundnut or sunflower oil
2 fat garlic cloves, thinly sliced
1 small red pepper, cored, seeded and thinly sliced
200g pack raw peeled tiger prawns, defrosted and patted dry if frozen
2 tbsp soy or fish sauce
100g/4oz bag baby spinach leaves

Takes 10 minutes • Serves 2

1 Heat a wok until you can feel a good heat rising. Add 2 tablespoons of oil and, a few seconds later, the sliced garlic. Stir fry until they start to turn golden, then, using a slotted spoon, spoon onto kitchen paper to drain.
2 Toss in the pepper and stir fry for 1 minute or so until softened, then scoop out and set aside. Add the remaining tablespoon of oil. Heat, then toss in the prawns and stir fry for another 2–3 minutes until cooked and beginning to brown. Splash in the soy or fish sauce.
3 Throw in the spinach and stir fry until it begins to wilt. Return the pepper and crisp garlic to the wok to warm through, then serve immediately.

• Per serving 269 kcalories, protein 21g, carbohydrate 7g, fat 18g, saturated fat 3g, fibre 2g, added sugar none, salt 3.38g

This superhealthy stew is even tastier topped
off with some crumbled feta cheese

Italian-style Beef Stew

½ onion, sliced
1 garlic clove, sliced
1 tbsp olive oil
150g pack beef stir-fry strips (or use beef steak, thinly sliced)
1 yellow pepper, seeded and thinly sliced
½ × 400g can chopped tomatoes
sprig fresh rosemary, chopped
handful of pitted olives

Takes 30 minutes • Serves 2

1 In a large saucepan, cook the onion and garlic in olive oil for 5 minutes until softened and turning golden.
2 Tip in the beef strips, pepper, tomatoes and rosemary, then bring to the boil. Simmer for 15 minutes until the meat is cooked through, adding some boiling water if needed.
3 Stir through the olives and serve with mash or polenta.

• Per serving 210 kcalories, protein 19.3g, carbohydrate 9.4g, fat 10.9g, saturated fat 2.3g, fibre 3.3g, added sugar none, salt 1.33g

Jazz up a basic shop-bought pizza
with this tasty topping.

Spicy Sausage and Chilli Pizza

1 thin-crust bought cheese and
tomato pizza
70g pack sliced chorizo
175g/6oz roasted red peppers, from
a jar or the deli, drained
and sliced
generous pinch crushed dried
chillies
50g/2oz grated cheddar
few black olives

Takes 20–30 minutes • Serves 2

1 Preheat the oven to the temperature recommended on the pizza pack. Unwrap the pizza, then scrunch up the slices of chorizo and arrange on top of the pizza with the sliced peppers.
2 Sprinkle over the chilli flakes and cheese then scatter with the olives so all of the ingredients give a generous, even covering.
3 Bake the pizza according to the pack instructions – about 15 minutes – until the cheese is melted and golden.

• Per serving 792 kcalories, protein 36.2g, carbohydrate 59.3g, fat 47.3g, saturated fat 17.3g, fibre 5.5g, added sugar none, salt 4.14g

This is a great feelgood lunch or light supper dish.
It's delicious served with a tomato and leaf salad.

Luscious Leek Omelette

1 tbsp olive oil
knob of butter
1 large leek, trimmed, sliced and washed
4 eggs, beaten
100g/4oz Caerphilly or Wensleydale

Takes 10–15 minutes • Serves 2

1 Heat the oil in a large frying pan for a few seconds, then drop in the butter. When the butter stops foaming, toss in the leek and stir fry for 4 minutes or until soft, but not coloured.
2 Pour in the eggs so they cover the bottom of the pan, add seasoning if you want, and cook for 3–5 minutes or until the eggs are no longer runny.
3 Crumble over the cheese, leave to cook for another minute, then fold the omelette in half. Cut into wedges to serve.

• Per serving 448 kcalories, protein 28g, carbohydrate 2g, fat 37g, saturated fat 16g, fibre 2g, added sugar none, salt 1.09g

A quick and utterly delicious version of a classic partnership.

Grilled Duck Breast with Minted Peas

about 15 fresh mint leaves, chopped
50g/2oz unsalted butter, softened
2 duck breasts, ideally Barbary or
Gressingham
dried herbes de Provence or dried
thyme or oregano
250g/9oz shelled garden peas,
about 800g/1lb12oz in their pods
buttered new potatoes, to serve

Takes 25–35 minutes • Serves 2

1 Blend the mint and butter. Pat the duck dry with kitchen paper and place on the oiled rack of a grill pan. Score the skin in a diamond pattern. Sprinkle with some salt and the dried herbs.
2 Preheat the grill to very hot. Grill the duck breasts skin-side up for 10 minutes (watch carefully as the fat can splatter) until the skin is browning and has yielded most of its fat – carefully pour this off. Turn the duck over and grill it on the flesh side for 5–10 minutes, depending on how rare you like it. Turn off the heat and let the duck rest.
3 Meanwhile, cook the peas in boiling salted water for 3–5 minutes until just tender. Drain, return to the hot pan and toss with the mint butter.
4 Serve the duck with the peas, and buttered new potatoes.

• Per serving 742 kcalories, protein 40g, carbohydrate 15g, fat 59g, saturated fat 24g, fibre 6g, added sugar none, salt 0.61g

Duck legs are perfect for slow-roasting – the flesh falls off the bones and the fat is released into the gravy to add body and flavour.

Roast Duck with Wine Sauce

2 duck legs
small bunch of rosemary sprigs
2 fat garlic cloves
¼ tsp five-spice powder
¼ bottle of red wine
1 tbsp redcurrant or quince jelly

Takes 1¼ hours • Serves 2

1 Preheat the oven to 190°C/Gas 5/fan oven 170°C. Put the duck legs in one layer in a small roasting tin on a bed of the rosemary sprigs and garlic cloves. Sprinkle with salt and the five-spice powder. Roast for 1 hour.

2 Bring the wine and jelly to a gentle simmer, stirring to dissolve the jelly, then continue to simmer for 4 minutes.

3 When the duck has been cooking for 1 hour remove from the oven and spoon off almost all the fat (save it for roast potatoes), then pour the wine mixture around it and return to the oven for a further 10–15 minutes to finish cooking the duck and reduce the sauce.

• Per serving 375 kcalories, protein 36.3g, carbohydrate 5g, fat 15.4g, saturated fat 4.3g, fibre none, added sugar 3.2g, salt 0.77g

This unusual bean mash, flavoured with horseradish, is the perfect accompaniment to beef. Serve with a big red wine.

Seared Beef with Bean Mash

4 tbsp extra-virgin olive oil
1 tbsp each chopped fresh rosemary and thyme
280g/9½oz piece beef fillet, trimmed
50g/2oz unsalted butter
1 large onion, finely chopped
2 garlic cloves, crushed
410g can cannellini beans, drained and rinsed
¼ small Savoy cabbage (about 200g/8oz), cored and shredded
3 tbsp chicken stock or water
1 tbsp finely grated horseradish (from a jar is fine)
3 tbsp chopped fresh flatleaf parsley
about 2 tbsp basil or olive oil, for drizzling

Takes 40 minutes, plus 2 hours or overnight chilling • Serves 2

1 Mix 2 tablespoons of the oil with rosemary, thyme and some pepper, in a shallow dish. Coat the beef in it, cover and chill for 2 hours or overnight.
2 Let beef come to room temperature. Heat a cast iron griddle pan until very hot. Wipe the beef, and cook 4–6 minutes on each side for rare. Rest for 15 minutes. Heat 1 tablespoon of oil and half the butter in a pan. Gently cook the onion and garlic for 8–10 minutes until soft, not brown. Add beans and cook for 1–2 minutes.
3 Heat a wok or large pan. Add remaining oil and butter. Stir fry the cabbage for 1–2 minutes. Add stock, season. Cook for a few more minutes to evaporate most of the liquid. Stir horseradish into the beans and mash. Stir in the parsley and season. Carve the beef into 4 slices. Serve with beans and cabbage, drizzled with oil.

• Per serving 890 kcalories, protein 44g, carbohydrate 36g, fat 65g, saturated fat 21g, fibre 12g, added sugar none, salt 0.83g

Half steak, half roast, this main course just oozes fine dining.

Succulent Sirloin and Tender Shallots

400g/14oz–500g/1lb 2oz sirloin steak in one piece (you can order from a butcher with some warning)
1–2 tbsp cracked black pepper
1 tbsp vegetable oil
small knob of butter
6 small shallots, peeled, halved, but still attached at root
1 fresh thyme sprig
1 bay leaf
glass of red wine (about 175ml/6fl oz)
100ml/3½fl oz beef stock
buttered green beans and roasted new potatoes with thyme, to serve

Takes 50 minutes–1 hour • Serves 2

1 Preheat oven to 220°C/Gas 7/fan oven 200°C. Season the steak with black pepper and some salt. Heat oil, then butter, in a heavy-based pan. Sear the steak for 1–2 minutes on each of its 6 sides. Remove to a shallow roasting tin, and lower heat under pan.
2 Sizzle the shallots in the pan for 6–8 minutes until softening. Add thyme and bay, turn up the heat and add the wine. Bubble and stir for about 5 minutes until reduced to a sticky glaze. Add the stock and bring to a boil. Tip sauce into a small saucepan and set aside.
3 Tip steak juices into the sauce. Roast the steak for 15 minutes for rare, 20 for medium, 30 for well done. Rest steak on a board for 5 minutes. Pour juices from the roasting tin into the sauce and gently reheat. Carve the steak thickly. Serve with shallots, beans and potatoes.

• Per serving 496 kcalories. protein 47g, carbohydrate 6g, fat 25g, saturated fat 9g, fibre none, added sugar none, salt 0.58g

A fail-safe recipe for classic steak and chips –
a real spoil-yourself supper.

Steak with Chunky Chips

500g/1lb 2oz floury potatoes
olive oil, for drizzling
2 thick sirloin steaks
100g/4oz crème fraîche
1–2 tbsp horseradish, depending on
how hot you like it
2 tbsp snipped fresh chives

Takes 1 hour • Serves 2

1 Preheat the oven to 200°C/Gas 6/fan oven 180°C. Cut the potatoes into chunky chips, leaving the skin on. Dry with kitchen paper, then tip into a roasting tin. Drizzle over 2 tablespoons of olive oil and shake the tin to coat the potatoes. Sprinkle with pepper and roast for 40–45 minutes, shaking the tin halfway through the cooking time. Season with salt when they are cooked.
2 Season the steaks and rub with olive oil. Mix the crème fraîche, horseradish and half the chives, salt and pepper.
3 When the chips are almost done, heat the grill to high and grill the steaks for 2–3 minutes on each side, depending on how you like them, and on their thickness. Serve with a pile of chips, a dollop of horseradish cream and a green salad with the remaining chives.

• Per serving 417 kcalories, protein 19g, carbohydrate 47g, fat 18g, saturated fat 9g, fibre 2g, added sugar none, salt 2.17g

An autumn supper for a cosy night at home.
Try serving with cider, which works well with the apples.

Pork with Frizzled Sage

3 small parsnips, trimmed, cut into
even chunks
3 tbsp olive oil
85g/3oz Gruyère cheese, cut in
2 slices
250g/9oz pork fillet (thick end), cut
in half, then sliced through each
half (but not all the way), so it can
be opened like a book
1 tbsp chopped fresh sage, plus
6 leaves
2 knobs of butter
2 small Cox's apples, cored
and sliced
½ small Savoy cabbage, cored
and finely shredded
small wine glass of dry white wine
or cider

Takes 1–1¼ hours • Serves 2

1 Preheat oven to 180°C/Gas 4/fan oven 160°C. Toss parsnips in 2 tablespoons of oil in a roasting tin and roast for 20 minutes. Put a slice of cheese in each opened piece of pork, sprinkle with chopped sage, season. Close pork, tying with string to make 2 parcels.
2 Heat remaining oil with half the butter in a pan, brown pork for 2–3 minutes each side. Lay pork on top of parsnips, roast for 20–25 minutes.
3 Meanwhile, heat remaining butter, fry sage leaves 30 seconds until crisp then remove. Fry apples in same pan until caramelised. Remove, add cabbage and stir fry until tender. Arrange cabbage, pork and apples on plates. Reduce the wine or cider in roasting tin for 3–4 minutes, pour around meat and scatter with sage leaves.

• Per serving 705 kcalories, protein 44g, carbohydrate 30g, fat 42g, saturated fat 16g, fibre 11g, added sugar 1g, salt 1.08g

An unusual, but delicious, treat for two. Choose a highly aromatic gin to complement the simplicity of the pork.

Pork with Gin and Coriander Sauce

4 tbsp gin, warmed
2 juniper berries, crushed
1 garlic clove, finely chopped
1 sprig fresh rosemary, finely chopped
1 tsp coriander seeds
3 tbsp olive oil
2 × 175g/6oz thick, boneless pork steaks, trimmed
150ml/¼ pint English apple juice, (the cloudy varieties have more flavour)
4 tbsp crème fraîche
mashed potato and buttered Savoy cabbage, to serve

Takes 35–45 minutes, plus soaking and marinating time • Serves 2

1 Pour the warm gin over the juniper berries. Soak for 20 minutes, then drain, reserving the gin. Pound the garlic, rosemary, coriander seeds, juniper berries and 2 tablespoons of olive oil. Spread this mixture over the pork. Cover and marinate (preferably overnight).

2 Heat the remaining oil in a small non-stick frying pan until very hot. Cook the pork quickly on both sides until golden. Pour in the gin – boil fast until it disappears. Pour in the apple juice. Scrape the pan to loosen any bits.

3 Simmer for 10 minutes until the pork is cooked and the sauce reduced but not too thick. Remove the pork to a warm plate. Swirl the crème fraîche into the sauce and boil rapidly for 1–2 minutes until syrupy, then season. Serve with mashed potatoes and buttered Savoy cabbage with sliced garlic.

• Per serving 557 kcalories, protein 41g, carbohydrate 10g, fat 32g, saturated fat 10g, fibre none, added sugar none, salt 0.35g

When the winter winds are howling, shut out the cold, light the fire and cosy up with this one-pot feast that's ideal for sharing.

Lamb with Lemon and Dill

350g/12oz ready-diced lamb
2 tsp plain flour
1 tbsp sunflower oil
1 onion, chopped
300ml/½ pint hot chicken or vegetable stock (a cube or powder is fine)
3 tbsp chopped fresh dill
1 bay leaf
300g/10oz salad potatoes, thickly sliced
zest and juice of ½ lemon
2 tbsp crème fraîche (half-fat is fine)

Takes 1¼ hours • Serves 2

1 Toss the lamb in the flour with a little salt and plenty of freshly ground black pepper. Heat the oil in a heavy-based pan, add the onion and fry for about 5 minutes until softened. Add the lamb and stir well until tinged brown.

2 Stir in the stock, 2 tablespoons of the dill and the bay leaf. Bring to the boil, then simmer for 30 minutes.

3 Add the potatoes and lemon juice and cook for a further 30 minutes until the potatoes are tender. Serve in soup plates or individual dishes with a spoonful of crème fraîche and a scattering of lemon zest and dill on each serving. Some crusty bread on the side will be useful for mopping up all the juices.

• Per serving 531 kcalories, protein 41g, carbohydrate 34g, fat 27g, saturated fat 11g, fibre 3g, added sugar none, salt 0.86g

A rack of lamb is a great idea for two people – you can buy a ready-trimmed rack from the chilled section of larger supermarkets.

Moroccan Spiced Rack of Lamb

5 tbsp olive oil
1–1½ tbsp harissa paste
¼ tsp cumin
¼ tsp turmeric
¼ tsp paprika
¼ tsp ground coriander
20g pack fresh flatleaf parsley, chopped
juice of ½ small lemon
1 rack of lamb (6–8 cutlets)
2 carrots, peeled and cut into chunks
100g/4oz couscous
150ml/¼ pint vegetable stock
juice of 1 satsuma
¼ tsp ground allspice
½ × 20g pack fresh mint, chopped
½ red onion, finely chopped
Greek yogurt and 50g/2oz flaked almonds, toasted, to serve

Takes 40–45 minutes • Serves 2

1 Preheat oven to 220°C/Gas 7/fan oven 200°C. Mix 2 tablespoons of the oil with the harissa, cumin, turmeric, paprika, coriander, half the parsley, lemon juice and a pinch of salt. Season lamb, spread with spice mix then roast for 15–20 minutes for rare–medium, 25 minutes for well done.

2 Meanwhile, toss carrots in a small roasting tin, with a pinch of salt and 1 tablespoon of the oil. Roast for 15 minutes. Meanwhile, tip couscous into bowl, pour over hot stock and let stand for 5 minutes. Stir and cool. Stir in remaining oil, parsley, satsuma juice, allspice, mint, onion, carrots and season.

3 Rest lamb for 5 minutes. Slice in half to give 3–4 cutlets each, then halve again. Serve with the yogurt and couscous scattered with almonds.

• Per serving 888 kcalories, protein 34g, carbohydrate 40g, fat 67g, saturated fat 18g, fibre 5g, added sugar none, salt 1.22g

So simple, but packed with flavour, this dish is great for two people to prepare and eat together.

Pepper Chicken Potato Crush

3 plump garlic cloves, peeled
3 tbsp chopped fresh flatleaf parsley
3 tbsp olive oil
2 boneless, skinless chicken breasts, preferably organic
100g goat's cheese (Capricorn is good), cut into 6 rounds
3 strips of roasted peppers in oil, drained, each cut in half
a few fresh thyme sprigs
300g/10oz small new potatoes
85g pack rocket or watercress, tough stems removed

Takes 55 minutes • Serves 2

1 Preheat oven to 200°C/Gas 6/fan oven 180°C. Soften the garlic in a little simmering water for 4–5 minutes. Drain and chop. Mix with the parsley and 1 tablespoon of oil. Make 3 deep diagonal slits across each breast. Reserve half the garlic mixture and spread the rest over the chicken and into the slits.
2 Halve each cheese slice and tuck two halves, a piece of pepper and some thyme into each slit. Season and bake in an oiled shallow dish for 30 minutes, until chicken is cooked.
3 Meanwhile, cook the potatoes for about 15 minutes. Drain, return to the pan and coarsely crush with a fork. Stir in rocket or watercress to leave to wilt. Stir remaining oil into the garlic mixture, season and stir into the potatoes. Serve with the chicken and any chicken juices.

• Per serving 562 kcalories, protein 46g, carbohydrate 30g, fat 29g, saturated fat 3g, fibre 4g, added sugar none, salt 0.88g

This is a substantial dish, so all you need to add to make a meal of it is tagliatelle or new potatoes.

Chicken with Grainy Mustard Sauce

2 boneless, skinless chicken breasts (about 300g/10oz total weight), preferably free-range
6 rashers of unsmoked streaky bacon, without rind
250g/9oz ready-washed spinach leaves, tough stalks removed
60g firm (not soft) goat's cheese, such as Crottin de Chavignol, cut in small cubes
2 tbsp olive oil
200ml/7fl oz vegetable or chicken stock
200ml/7fl oz dry white wine
½ × 200ml tub (or 4 heaped tbsp) crème fraîche
1 heaped tsp wholegrain mustard
tagliatelle or new potatoes, to serve

Takes 1–1¼ hours • Serves 2

1 Flatten each breast to 1½ times its original width. Overlap and stretch 3 bacon rashers on a board into a rectangle. Lay a breast on top, repeat with remaining bacon and chicken. Cover each with 4 spinach leaves, flatten. Put cheese along the middle. Season with pepper. Roll each one up, secure with cocktail sticks.
2 Heat half the oil in a frying pan. Cook the chicken over a high heat for 3–4 minutes until bacon is golden. Turn, cook for 3–4 minutes more. Add stock and wine. Simmer for 20 minutes, turning chicken halfway. Remove chicken, stir in crème fraîche and mustard.
3 Heat remaining oil in a large pan, add remaining spinach, season. Cover and cook for 2 minutes to wilt the spinach. Squeeze well. Serve each breast, halved, with the sauce and tagliatelle or new potatoes.

• Per serving 773 kcalories, protein 58g, carbohydrate 5g, fat 51g, saturated fat 23g, fibre 3g, added sugar none, salt 3.59g

Try adding lightly oiled cherry tomatoes, halved red onions and lemons to the barbecue for the last 10 minutes, to serve with the chicken.

Spatchcock Barbecue Chicken

1.3kg/3lb chicken, spatchcocked
a little beer or water, to baste
1–2 lemons, quartered, to serve

FOR THE MARINADE
3 tbsp olive oil, plus extra to serve
1 tsp paprika, plus extra to serve
1 garlic clove, crushed
zest and juice of 1 lemon

Takes 1 hour, plus marinating •
Serves 2

1 Make the marinade. Mix together the oil, paprika, garlic, lemon zest and some salt and pepper. Brush this all over the skin of the spatchcock chicken and marinate in the fridge for 30 minutes.

2 To cook on a barbecue: preheat the barbecue. Cook for 5 minutes each side in the centre, then draw aside to the edges to cook on a gentler heat. Turn regularly. Baste in between with beer or water. To check that the chicken is cooked through, pierce with a knife between the thighs and breast bone: the flesh should be white and firm.

3 Remove from the heat and leave to rest, covered with foil, for 10–15 minutes. Cut into portions, drizzle over the lemon juice and seasoning, plus a little oil and pinches of paprika. Serve with lemon quarters.

• Per serving 650 kcalories, protein 59g, carbohydrate 1g, fat 45g, saturated fat 14g, fibre 1g, added sugar none, salt 0.91g

A fresh and tasty idea for bringing summer into your home
at any time of year – perfect for a candlelit supper.

Mediterranean Salad Tarts

2 large onions, thinly sliced
knob of butter
2 tbsp olive oil, plus extra
1 tsp light muscovado sugar
6 medium new potatoes
250g ready-made puff pastry,
thawed if frozen
200g/8oz cherry tomatoes on
the vine
100g/4oz camembert, cut into slices
6 anchovy fillets
6 black olives, not pitted
1 tbsp good-quality pesto
50g/2oz rocket leaves
100g/4oz green beans, lightly
steamed
good squeeze of lemon juice
a few fresh basil leaves, roughly torn

Takes 55 minutes • Serves 2

1 Fry onions slowly in butter and half the oil for 15–20 minutes until soft and golden. Stir in the sugar, cook 3–4 minutes. Remove and cool.
2 Cook potatoes in boiling water for 10 minutes or until tender. Drain, cool and slice.
3 Preheat the oven to 220°C/Gas 7/fan oven 200°C. Halve the pastry, roll into 2 18cm/7in rounds. Put each round on a baking sheet and spread the onions over. Reserve 2 sprigs of tomatoes and halve the others. Lay the cheese, sliced potatoes, tomatoes and anchovies over the onions. Top each tart with a tomato sprig, olives and an extra drizzle of oil. Bake for 15–20 minutes until golden.
4 Mix pesto with remaining oil. Toss rocket and beans with lemon juice and extra oil. Season. Drizzle pesto over the tarts, scatter with basil leaves. Serve with the rocket salad.

• Per serving 1025 kcalories, protein 28g, carbohydrate 93g, fat 63g, saturated fat 13g, fibre 7g, added sugar 3g, salt 3.49g

Baking the trout in a foil parcel keeps it nice and moist and the chicory infuses it with a slightly nutty taste.

Baked Trout with Chicory and Bacon

4 trout fillets, skin on (about 140g/5oz each)
50g/2oz butter, softened
1 tbsp Dijon mustard
20g pack fresh flatleaf parsley, chopped
2 shallots, finely chopped
6 garlic cloves, crushed
juice of 1 lemon
3 heads of chicory
50g/2oz dry-cured streaky bacon, chopped
25g/1oz roasted, skinned hazelnuts, chopped
olive oil and lemon wedges, to serve

Takes 35–40 minutes • Serves 2

1 Preheat oven to 200°C/Gas 6/fan oven 180°C. Make 3 slashes in skin of each fillet. Mix half the butter with mustard, parsley, shallots, garlic and lemon juice. Rub over fish and into the slashes.

2 Keeping a few chicory leaves back, divide the rest between 2 large sheets of foil. Lay one fillet, skin-side down, on each pile of chicory. Top with second fillet, skin-side up. Season. Loosely wrap foil around, seal the edges. Put parcels on a baking sheet. Bake 15 minutes.

3 Meanwhile, melt remaining butter in small frying pan. Fry bacon and hazelnuts until golden. Transfer fish and chicory to plates, drizzling over the juices and a splash of oil. Garnish with reserved chicory scattered with bacon and hazelnuts. Serve with lemon wedges.

• Per serving 707 kcalories, protein 63g, carbohydrate 9g, fat 47g, saturated fat 19g, fibre 4g, added sugar none, salt 2.26g

The simplest coating for fried fish is seasoned flour,
as in this popular French classic.

Sole Meunière

3 tbsp plain flour
2 sole or plaice fillets, skin on (about
140g/5oz each)
1½ tbsp light olive or sunflower oil
25g/1oz butter, ideally unsalted
juice of ½ lemon
1 tbsp small capers (optional)

Takes 15 minutes • Serves 2

1 In a large shallow bowl, season the flour
with a little salt and pepper. Toss the fish in
the flour, coating well, and shake off any
excess.

2 Heat the oil in a large frying pan. Add the
fish and cook, skin-side down, for 2 minutes.
Use a fish slice or a large spatula to turn,
then cook the other side for 1–2 minutes
until golden.

3 Remove the fish to a warmed plate, then
season. Wipe out the pan with kitchen
paper. Return the pan to the heat, then add
the butter. Heat until it melts and begins to
turn a light brown, then mix in the lemon
juice and capers, if using. Swirl in the pan for
a few seconds, return the fish to the pan
and spoon over any juices.

• Per serving 361 kcalories, protein 26.6g,
carbohydrate 17.7g, fat 20.9g, saturated fat 8.4g,
fibre 0.7g, added sugar none, salt 0.53g

Try this creative oriental salmon supper
when you want a treat.

Salmon Teriyaki with Crispy Ginger

1 tbsp vegetable or groundnut oil,
plus extra
2 salmon fillets, each about
140g/5oz, preferably organic
(skin on or off)
8 × 5cm/2in long slices fresh root
ginger, cut into very thin strips
149g/5oz Thai or basmati rice
1 tsp sesame oil
250g/9oz asparagus, trimmed
1 tbsp sesame seeds, toasted (in a
dry pan over a medium heat for
about a minute, shaking often)

FOR THE MARINADE
3 tbsp Japanese soy sauce
1 tbsp clear honey
2 tbsp dry sherry
1 small garlic clove, crushed

Takes 30–35 minutes, plus one hour
marinating • Serves 2

1 Mix marinade ingredients in shallow dish.
Coat salmon in marinade, cover, chill for 1 hour.
2 Heat about 1cm/½ in oil in a small pan.
Fry the ginger for about 1 minute until crispy.
Remove and drain on paper towels. Set aside.
3 Ten minutes before serving, cook the rice
in unsalted boiling water. Meanwhile, heat
the tablespoon of vegetable oil in a frying
pan. Reserving the marinade, fry the salmon
for 3–5 minutes on each side. Mix the
sesame oil with a teaspoon of vegetable oil.
Steam the asparagus for 3–5 minutes, then
toss in the oil mixture. Simmer the marinade
in a pan for less than a minute to reduce
slightly. Drain the rice, stir in the sesame
seeds. Sit the salmon on the asparagus,
pour over the sauce, top with the ginger and
serve with the rice.

• Per serving 682 kcalories, protein 40g, carbohydrate
71g, fat 27g, saturated fat 4g, fibre 3g, added sugar
8g, salt 6.96g

Fresh mussels are surprisingly quick and easy to prepare.
Serve this dish with bread to mop up the delicious juices.

Mussels with Wine and Smoky Bacon

200g/8oz new potatoes, halved
350g/12oz, about ½ small Savoy
cabbage, cored and shredded
1 tbsp olive or sunflower oil
1 small onion, finely chopped
1 plump garlic clove, crushed
200ml/7fl oz dry white wine
2 fresh thyme sprigs
1 bay leaf
1kg/2lb 4oz fresh mussels, well
scrubbed and beards removed
(discard any that are open or
don't close when tapped)
100g/4oz smoked streaky bacon,
chopped
2 tbsp double cream

Takes about 50 minutes • Serves 2

1 Cook potatoes in boiling salted water for 10–12 minutes until tender, adding the cabbage for the last 2 minutes. Meanwhile, heat oil in a saucepan, fry the onion and garlic for 2 minutes. Add wine and herbs, season with pepper. Bring to the boil, tip in mussels and cover tightly. Cook for 5–8 minutes, shaking the pan often, until they open.
2 Meanwhile, dry-fry bacon until crisp. Drain on kitchen paper. Drain the potatoes and cabbage. When mussels open, put a colander over a saucepan and tip in the mussels and liquid. Discard herbs and any unopened mussels.
3 Warm the cooking liquid and stir in the cream. Season. Spoon the potatoes and cabbage into bowls, top with the mussels and bacon, then the cooking liquid.

• Per serving 553 kcalories, protein 32.4g, carbohydrate 34.3g, fat 29.3g, saturated fat 10.4g, fibre 7g, added sugar 0.7g, salt 2.78g

Steaming is a great way of cooking food with flavourings. The results are light and tasty and retain all the freshness of the ingredients.

Summer Vegetable Bowl

1–2 carrots, cut into stick if large
1–2 turnips, cut into wedges
1 tbsp dry sherry
2 tbsp soy sauce
1 medium courgette, cut into
1cm/½in slices
4–6 short asparagus spears
3 fresh shiitake or open-cup
mushrooms, sliced in 4
25g/1oz butter
2 spring onions, shredded
100g/4oz smoked tofu, cubed
(optional)

Takes 25 minutes • Serves 2

1 Mix together the carrot and turnip, then marinade with the sherry and soy sauce for about 10 minutes in a heatproof shallow bowl that will fit inside a steamer basket.
2 Bring a pan of water to the boil, fit the steamer basket, place the bowl inside, cover and steam for 4–5 minutes. Add the courgette slices, asparagus and mushrooms, stirring to mix. Dot with the butter, sprinkle with the spring onions, cover and continue steaming for another 3 minutes.
3 Add the tofu, if using, and continue steaming for 2 minutes. Remove the bowl and mix everything together one more time.

• Per serving 185 kcalories, protein 5g, carbohydrate 14g, fat 12g, saturated fat 7g, fibre 6g, added sugar 1g, salt 2.99g

Microwaving the rice is a fantastic short-cut option for stress-free cooking.

Oriental Rice Express

2 tbsp olive oil
1 large onion, chopped into chunks
½ tsp Chinese five-spice powder or ground ginger
300–340g pack fresh stir-fry vegetables (such as sliced water chestnuts, mushrooms, pak choi and beansprouts)
2 × 250g packets ready-cooked express basmati rice
2 tbsp soy sauce, or more to taste

Takes 15–25 minutes • Serves 2

1 Heat the wok, pour in the oil and heat it up. Add the onion and cook, stirring occasionally, until it starts to brown. Sprinkle in the five-spice powder or ginger and stir fry for 30 seconds. Stir in the vegetables, keeping the heat quite high. Stir fry for 4–5 minutes until the vegetables begin to soften, but stay crunchy.

2 While the vegetables cook, make a 2.5cm/1in tear in the top of each rice packet. Microwave each packet separately for 2 minutes on high. (If you don't have a microwave, cook the rice according to the pack instructions before you heat up the wok.)

3 Splash in the soy sauce, and remove from the heat. For more sauce, splash in 1–2 tablespoons of water. Serve rice topped with the vegetables.

• Per serving 503 kcalories, protein 12g, carbohydrate 85g, fat 15g, saturated fat 2g, fibre 5g, added sugar none, salt 2.75g

These stuffed onions make an excellent vegetarian main course with a rice or couscous pilaf and a crisp salad.

Feta-stuffed Roasty Onions

2 medium onions
2 tbsp olive oil, plus extra for drizzling
4 thyme sprigs

FOR THE STUFFING
200g block of feta, crumbled
50g/2oz white or brown breadcrumbs
1 fresh red chilli, seeded and finely chopped
6 pieces of sun-dried tomato in olive oil, drained and chopped
large pinch chopped fresh thyme leaves
2 tbsp chopped fresh parsley
50g/2oz walnut pieces, chopped
1 medium egg, beaten

Takes about 1½ hours • Serves 2

1 Preheat oven to 190°C/Gas 5/fan oven 170°C. Keeping them whole, peel the onions, discarding the first layer as you peel. Halve the onions widthways and spoon out several layers from each centre. Use bits of the centre layers (sliced) to fill any holes. Put onions, cut side up, in a small ovenproof dish. Add a splash of water, brush them with some oil. Cover, bake for 40–45 minutes until tender.
2 Meanwhile, chop the inner layers. Heat remaining oil, fry the onion, stirring occasionally, for 10 minutes until softened. Cool, then mix in a bowl with half the feta and remaining stuffing ingredients. Season.
3 Increase oven to 200°C/Gas 6/fan oven 180°C. Divide stuffing between onions. Scatter over remaining cheese and thyme sprigs. Drizzle with oil and cook for 25 minutes.

• Per serving 742 kcalories, protein 28g, carbohydrate 35g, fat 55g, saturated fat 17g, fibre 5g, added sugar none, salt 5g

Any leftovers are delicious served cold for lunch.

Griddled Halloumi with Spiced Couscous

1 head of broccoli
handful of sugar snap peas
175g/6oz couscous
½ tsp each cinnamon, cumin and coriander
300ml/½ pint hot vegetable stock
250g pack halloumi cheese
handful of cherry tomatoes, halved
juice of ½ lemon
drizzle of olive oil
small handful of fresh coriander leaves, chopped

Takes 20 minutes • Serves 2

1 Cut the broccoli into florets and thickly slice the stalk. Pour boiling water into a steamer. Steam the broccoli for 6 minutes. Add the peas and steam for 2 minutes more.
2 Meanwhile, mix the couscous with the spices in a bowl, pour over the hot stock, then cover and leave to stand for 5 minutes.
3 Heat a non-stick frying pan or griddle pan. Cut the halloumi into 6–8 slices and cook quickly on each side for 2 minutes until lightly tinged brown.
4 Mix the vegetables and tomatoes into the couscous, fork in the lemon juice, oil and coriander. Pile onto two plates and top with the halloumi.

• Per serving 711 kcalories, protein 40g, carbohydrate 52g, fat 39g, saturated fat 19g, fibre 5g, added sugar none, salt 5.12g

The different flavours in each mouthful make this dish irresistible.
Serve for supper or for lunch as an alternative to soup or a sandwich.

Tamarind Chickpeas

1 tbsp vegetable or sunflower oil
¼ tsp nigella seeds (look for these
in supermarkets)
1½ tsp fennel seeds
1 medium onion, chopped
400g can chopped tomatoes
3 fresh green chillies, seeded and
cut into quarters lengthways
2–3 tsp light muscovado sugar
1 tsp paprika
1 tsp turmeric
410g can chickpeas, drained and
rinsed
1 tbsp tamarind paste
1 tbsp chopped fresh coriander
½ × 250g bag baby spinach leaves
natural yogurt and chapatis,
to serve

Takes 25–35 minutes • Serves 2

1 Heat the oil in a saucepan and fry the nigella and fennel seeds for about 10 seconds. Add the onion and cook gently for 8–10 minutes until golden.
2 Mix in the tomatoes, chillies, sugar, paprika, turmeric and chickpeas. Bring to the boil, then simmer for 10 minutes.
3 Stir in the tamarind and coriander. Add the spinach leaves and stir gently until they've just wilted. Serve with yogurt and chapatis.

• Per serving 334 kcalories, protein 16g, carbohydrate 45g, fat 11g, saturated fat 1g, fibre 9g, added sugar 5g, salt 1.34g

If you want a break from bread,
serve the lentils with rice instead.

Indian Beans on Toast

1 tbsp vegetable oil
1 medium onion, cut into thin wedges
½ tsp turmeric
½ rounded tsp ground cumin
2 medium tomatoes, cut into rough chunks
½ × 410g can green lentils, drained
1 plain or garlic and coriander naan
handful of fresh coriander leaves, roughly torn
yogurt and lemon wedges, to serve

Takes 20–30 minutes • Serves 2

1 Heat the oil in a frying pan. Tip in the onion and cook, stirring occasionally, until really golden (5–8 minutes). Stir in the turmeric and cumin for 1 minute to release their flavour. Add the tomatoes and cook briefly, gently stirring, until they just start to soften but don't lose their shape.

2 Tip the lentils into the pan and heat through. While they are warming, tear the naan bread roughly in half and toast under the grill or in the toaster just to warm through, but not brown.

3 Stir 2 tablespoons of water into the lentils to make a little sauce, then warm through. Add the coriander to the lentils, season with salt and serve spooned over the naan while hot, with a dollop of yogurt and a lemon wedge.

• Per serving 376 kcalories, protein 12.2g, carbohydrate 57.4g, fat 12.4g, saturated fat 3.3g, fibre 4.9g, added sugar 1.8g, salt 2.08g

A substantial, well-balanced and delicious supper
full of healthy ingredients.

Spinach with Coriander Couscous

1 tbsp olive oil
1 onion, roughly chopped
2 tsp ground coriander
½ tsp ground cumin
3 garlic cloves, crushed
2 tbsp tomato purée
410g can chickpeas in unsalted
water, drained
175g/6oz couscous
small bunch of fresh coriander,
finely chopped
300ml/½ pint hot vegetable stock
175g/6oz cherry tomatoes
250g bag baby leaf spinach

Takes 30–40 minutes • Serves 2

1 Heat the oil in a large saucepan and fry the onion until softened. Stir in the ground spices and garlic and fry for 2 minutes more. Stir in the tomato purée, chickpeas and 150ml/¼ pint water. Bring to the boil, cover and cook gently for 5 minutes.
2 Meanwhile, put the couscous and chopped coriander in a large heatproof bowl, pour the hot stock over and cover tightly with cling film. Leave for 10 minutes to absorb the liquid.
3 Tip the cherry tomatoes and spinach into the chickpeas. Stir until the spinach has wilted and the tomatoes softened, but still have their shape. Season with pepper. Fluff up the couscous grains with a fork. Taste and add salt only if needed (the stock is salty). Serve topped with the chickpeas and spinach.

• Per serving 624 kcalories, protein 26.3g, carbohydrate 96g, fat 17.3g, saturated fat 4g, fibre 15.7g, added sugar none, salt 0.95g

Try to buy mature cheddar for this dish –
it has loads of flavour so you don't have to use very much.

Potato Wedge Tortilla

1 tbsp sunflower oil
1 large potato, cut into 8 wedges
(no need to peel)
1 small onion, halved and sliced
1 red pepper, seeded and cut into
chunks
6 eggs
handful of grated cheddar cheese,
preferably mature

Takes 30–40 minutes • Serves 2

1 Heat the oil in a non-stick frying pan. Add the potato wedges and fry gently for 15–20 minutes, turning occasionally until golden and cooked through. Take the potato out of the pan, add the onion and fry until soft and golden. Add the red pepper and cook until softened. Return potatoes to the pan.
2 Beat the eggs with plenty of seasoning, then pour over the potato, pepper and onion. Push the egg mix around in the pan to make space for the uncooked egg to flow into.
3 When the egg looks quite set, throw the grated cheese over and put under a hot grill for a few minutes until the cheese is golden. Cut into wedges and serve. (Salad is good with this.)

• Per serving 467 kcalories, protein 28g, carbohydrate 23g, fat 30g, saturated fat 9g, fibre 2g, added sugar none, salt 0.89g

Omelettes don't have to be boring –
this version is suprisingly creamy and tasty with added spice.

Chilli Cheese Omelette

2 spring onions
handful of fresh coriander
4 large eggs
2 tbsp sunflower oil
1 tsp chopped fresh red chilli, or
2 generous pinches of dried
chilli flakes
50g/2oz mild grated cheddar

Takes 10 minutes • Serves 2

1 Chop the spring onions and coriander quite finely. Beat two of the eggs together with salt and pepper. Heat 1 tablespoon of the oil in a small frying pan then tip in half the onion, coriander and chilli and stir round the pan for a second or two so they soften a little. Pour in the eggs and keep them moving until two thirds have scrambled.
2 Settle the eggs back down on the base of the pan, scatter over half the cheese and cook for about 1 minute until the omelette is just set and the cheese has melted.
3 Carefully fold the omelette using a palette knife and slide from the pan to a serving plate. Serve while hot and the cheese is still melting. Repeat with the remaining ingredients to make another omelette.

• Per serving 387 kcalories, protein 21.7g, carbohydrate 0.4g, fat 33.2g, saturated fat 10.5g, fibre 0.1g, added sugar none, salt 0.89g

Roasting the squash brings out its sweet nutty flavour
and the onions add a savoury note.

Rigatoni with Roasted Squash

1 butternut squash, about
700g/1lb 9oz
2 red onions
2 garlic cloves, sliced
2 tbsp olive oil
175g/6oz rigatoni or penne
3 rounded tbsp crème fraîche
freshly grated vegetarian parmesan
cheese, to serve (optional)

Takes 50 minutes •
Serves 2 generously

1 Preheat the oven to 200°C/Gas 6/fan oven 180°C. Peel, halve and seed the squash, then cut into bite-size chunks and tip into a roasting tin. Peel the onions, leaving the roots intact, then cut each one lengthways into 8 wedges and add them to the tin with the garlic, oil and some seasoning. Toss until all the ingredients are glistening, then roast for 30 minutes.
2 Meanwhile, cook the pasta in salted boiling water for 8–10 minutes, or according to the pack instructions, until tender. Drain, reserving 4 tablespoons of the water.
3 Remove the tin from the oven and stir in the 4 tablespoons water and the crème fraîche, then toss in the pasta. Serve sprinkled with black pepper and parmesan if you like.

• Per serving 572 kcalories, protein 16.7g, carbohydrate 102g, fat 13.8g, saturated fat 7.6g, fibre 9.2g, added sugar none, salt 0.16g

Adapt this tasty and substantial winter soup according to what you've got in the freezer – try adding frozen broad beans, sweetcorn or spinach.

Storecupboard Minestrone

2 tbsp olive oil
1 onion, roughly chopped
2 × 400g cans chopped tomatoes
1 tbsp vegetable bouillon powder
(such as Marigold Swiss
vegetable bouillon)
1 tbsp pesto, plus extra to serve
pinch of sugar
50g/2oz dried mini pasta shapes for
soup (such as farfalline), or
spaghetti or other pasta, broken
into small pieces
410g can mixed pulses, drained
and rinsed
200g/8oz frozen green vegetables,
such as sliced green beans
and peas

Takes 30 minutes • Serves 2

1 Heat the oil in a large saucepan and cook the onion over a low heat until softened. Pour in the tomatoes and 4 canfuls of water. Sprinkle in the bouillon powder, then stir in the pesto, sugar and seasoning to taste.
2 Increase the heat and bring to the boil. Add the pasta and simmer for 10 minutes or until just tender, stirring occasionally.
3 Tip in the pulses and frozen vegetables, stir well and bring to the boil again. Cover and simmer for 10 minutes, stirring occasionally. Taste for seasoning. Serve with extra pesto.

• Per serving 256 kcalories, protein 12g, carbohydrate 33g, fat 9g, saturated fat 2g, fibre 9g, added sugar 1g, salt 2.16g

The lemon and mint make this
a perfect dish for a summer meal.

Spring-into-summer Pasta

175g/6oz tagliatelle
250g/9oz courgettes
½ × 190g pack fresh shelled peas,
or use frozen
zest and juice of ½ lemon
small handful of fresh mint leaves
chopped
½ × 250g tub ricotta
olive oil, for drizzling

Takes 15 minutes • Serves 2

1 Cook the tagliatelle according to the pack instructions. Meanwhile, cut the courgettes into thin finger-length sticks.
2 When the pasta has 2 minutes left to cook, tip the courgettes and peas into the pan, then cook until just tender. Drain and return to the pan.
3 Toss in the lemon zest and juice, most of the mint, then season to taste. Divide between two bowls, spoon small dollops of ricotta over each, sprinkle with the remaining mint and serve with a drizzle of oil and a grind of pepper.

• Per serving 486 kcalories, protein 22.1g, carbohydrate 75.6g, fat 12.7g, saturated fat 5.4g, fibre 6.1g, added sugar none, salt 0.19g

With just six ingredients, these tortilla wraps
are perfect picnic food.

Greek Salad Tortillas

2 very large soft tortilla wraps
1 large vine-ripened tomato, roughly
chopped
5cm/2in piece of cucumber, cut into
sticks
6 kalamata olives, stoned (optional)
50g/2oz feta cheese
2 heaped tbsp houmous

Takes 10 minutes • Serves 2

1 Heat the tortillas. If you have gas, put
each one for 10 seconds on a lit gas ring –
you have to be a little bit brave – then turn it
over quickly, using tongs, and heat the other
side for another 8 seconds or so. The
tortillas will be slightly charred in places.
If you don't have gas, warm a pan to a
medium heat before quickly tossing in your
tortillas one at a time. You don't need any oil.
2 Make a row of tomato, cucumber, feta
and olives down the centre of each warm
tortilla. Spread the houmous around the top
and sides of the tortillas. Fold in the sides to
seal in the ingredients and roll up tightly to
make a big cigar. Cut each in half and eat
with your fingers.

• Per serving 297 kcalories, protein 10g, carbohydrate
25g, fat 18g, saturated fat 5g, fibre 3g, added sugar
none, salt 2.08g

The sweet squash partners the chilli, spinach and cheese deliciously.

Spiced Butternut Squash with Cheese

1 heaped tsp coriander seeds
½ tsp crushed dried chilli flakes
½ tsp coarse sea salt
½ tsp black peppercorns
1 large butternut squash, peeled, seeded and cut into chunks
3 tbsp olive oil
4 garlic cloves, unpeeled and whole
225g bag baby spinach
225g/8oz Ardrahan (or other strong semi-soft cheese, rind removed), cut into slices

Takes 1¼ hours • Serves 2

1 Preheat the oven to 200°C/Gas 6/fan oven 180°C. Roughly crush the spices, salt and peppercorns using a pestle and mortar. Mix the squash and oil in a roasting tin, sprinkle over half the spice mix and tuck in the garlic.
2 Roast for 20 minutes, turn the squash over and dust with the rest of the spice mix. Roast for another 20 minutes.
3 Remove and peel the garlic, then return the cloves to the tin and stir in the spinach. Scatter over the cheese and return to the oven for 2–3 minutes or until the spinach has wilted and the cheese melted.

• Per serving 331 kcalories, protein 6.2g, carbohydrate 39g, fat 17.8g, saturated fat 2.4g, fibre 7.2g, added sugar none, salt 1.3g

All you need to serve with the plaice
is a bowl of hot buttered new potatoes.

Plaice in a Hot Vinaigrette

2 large plaice fillets, about
140g/5oz each, skin on
1½ tbsp olive oil
1 garlic clove, thinly sliced
1 leek, washed, trimmed and
shredded into very thin strips
juice of ½ lemon, plus wedges
boiled new potatoes, to serve

Takes 25–35 minutes • Serves 2

1 Preheat the grill to high. Lay the plaice fillets, skin-side down, on an oiled baking sheet, season with salt and freshly ground black pepper and drizzle with ½ tablespoon of the oil. Grill the fish for 2–3 minutes (no need to turn).

2 While the plaice is grilling, heat the remaining oil in a small frying pan. Add the garlic and leek and fry over a gentle heat until soft and golden. Pour in the lemon juice, then take the pan off the heat.

3 Remove the fish from under the grill and put on warm plates. Using a slotted spoon, top the fish with the garlicky leeks. Heat the vinaigrette left in the pan for a minute until piping hot, then pour it over the fish and season with pepper. Serve with lemon wedges and boiled new potatoes.

• Per serving 203 kcalories, protein 24.6g, carbohydrate 2.6g, fat 10.5g, saturated fat 1.5g, fibre 1.5g, added sugar none, salt 0.68g

Sensational for a light meal,
this broth is packed with flavour.

Teriyaki Chicken Noodle Broth

1.3 litres/2¼ pints hot vegetable stock (using Marigold Swiss vegetable bouillon)
½ tsp grated fresh root ginger
1 tbsp teriyaki marinade or light soy sauce
¼ tsp Chinese five-spice powder
50g/2oz fine egg or rice noodles
140g/5oz fresh stir-fry vegetables
50g/2oz mushrooms (any type), halved or sliced
85g/3oz skinless roast chicken, torn into shreds
½ tsp sesame seeds
chilli sauce, to serve

Takes 15–20 minutes • Serves 2

1 Pour the stock into a large pan and heat until just simmering. Stir in the ginger and teriyaki marinade or soy sauce and then add the five-spice powder.
2 Add your chosen noodles and cook for 3–4 minutes, giving them a gentle stir to loosen them up every now and then. Tip in the stir-fry vegetables and mushrooms. Cook for a couple of minutes, then add the cooked chicken and simmer for a further 1–2 minutes.
3 Season the soup to taste and ladle into warmed bowls. Sprinkle with sesame seeds. Serve with the chilli sauce.

• Per serving 238 kcalories, protein 18.2g, carbohydrate 25.3g, fat 7.8g, saturated fat 1.3g, fibre 2.4g, added sugar 0.2g, salt 2.07g

Serve with Thai jasmine rice. And if you have some sesame seeds, toast a handful and toss into the rice just before serving.

Thai-style Steamed Fish

2 trout fillets, each weighing about 140g/5oz
small knob of fresh root ginger, peeled and chopped
1 small garlic clove, chopped
1 small fresh red chilli (not bird's eye), seeded and finely chopped
grated zest and juice of 1 lime
3 baby pak choi, each quartered lengthways
2 tbsp soy sauce

Takes 25–30 minutes • Serves 2

1 Nestle the fish fillets side by side on a large square of foil and scatter the ginger, garlic, chilli and lime zest over them. Drizzle the lime juice on top, then scatter the pieces of pak choi around and on top of the fish.
2 Pour the soy sauce over the pak choi and loosely seal the foil to make a package, making sure you leave space at the top for the steam to circulate as the fish cooks.
3 Steam for 15 minutes. (If you haven't got a steamer, put the parcel on a heatproof plate over a pan of gently simmering water, cover with a lid and steam.)

• Per serving 199 kcalories, protein 29g, carbohydrate 4g, fat 7g, saturated fat 2g, fibre none, added sugar none, salt 3.25g

Swap the potatoes for sweet potatoes
for a more exotic flavour.

Healthy Fish and Chips

450g/1lb potatoes, peeled and cut into chips
1 tbsp olive oil, plus a little extra for brushing
2 skinless white fish fillets, about 140g/4oz each
grated zest and juice of 1 lemon
small handful of fresh flatleaf parsley leaves, chopped
1 tbsp capers, chopped
2 heaped tbsp fat-free Greek yogurt

Takes 40–45 minutes • Serves 2

1 Preheat the oven to 200°C/Gas 6/fan oven 180°C. Toss the chips in a tablespoon of oil. Spread over a baking sheet in an even layer and bake for 40 minutes until browned and crisp.

2 Put the fish in a shallow dish and brush lightly with oil, and some salt and pepper. Sprinkle with half the lemon juice and bake for 10 minutes. Sprinkle over a little of the parsley and the lemon zest and return to the oven for a further 3–5 minutes to finish cooking.

3 Meanwhile, mix the capers, yogurt, remaining parsley and lemon juice together, and season if you wish. Serve the chips with the fish and the yogurt mix.

• Per serving 373 kcalories, protein 35g, carbohydrate 41g, fat 9g, saturated fat 1g, fibre 3g, added sugar none, salt 0.96g

A glass of cold white wine, such as Sancerre, is the perfect accompaniment to this light supper dish.

Spaghetti alle Vongole

145g/5oz spaghetti
500g/1lb 2oz fresh clams in shells
2 ripe tomatoes
2 tbsp olive oil
1 fat garlic clove, chopped
1 small fresh red chilli, finely chopped
splash white wine (about half a small glass)
2 tbsp chopped parsley

Takes 20–25 minutes • Serves 2

1 Put the water for the spaghetti on to boil. Rinse the clams in several changes of cold water. Discard any that are open or damaged. Cover the tomatoes with boiling water, leave for 1 minute, then drain and slip off their skins. Remove the seeds and chop the flesh.
2 Cook spaghetti according to pack instructions. Meanwhile, heat the oil in a large pan, add the garlic and chilli, then fry gently for a few seconds. Stir in the tomatoes, then add the clams and splash of wine, salt and pepper, and bring to the boil. Cover and cook for 3–4 minutes, until clams open.
3 Drain pasta, then tip into pan with the parsley and toss together. Serve in bowls with bread for mopping up juices.

• Per serving 409 kcalories, protein 16g, carbohydrate 56g, fat 13g, saturated fat 2g, fibre 3g, added sugar none, salt 0.10g

Jumbo king prawns are ideal for quick cooking – just wrap in foil
and cook on the side of the barbecue until piping hot.

Chilli Prawns

300g/10oz jumbo king prawns
2 lemongrass stalks, bruised

FOR THE MARINADE
½ large fresh red chilli, seeded and
finely chopped
2 tsp olive oil
1 tsp fish sauce or soy sauce
1 plump garlic clove, crushed
1 tsp grated fresh root ginger
½ tsp ground cumin

Takes 15 minutes • Serves 2

1 Mix the marinade ingredients and add
to the prawns, rubbing it all over to coat.
Leave for 5 minutes.
2 To cook on a barbecue: thread the
prawns on metal skewers, place in the
centre of the preheated grill on the
lemongrass stems for fragrance, and cook
for 2–3 minutes, turning once until opaque.
3 Discard the lemongrass before eating.

• Per serving 122 kcalories, protein 26.6g,
carbohydrate 0.2g, fat 1.7g, saturated fat 0.3g,
fibre none, added sugar none, salt 0.85g

For a vegetarian version, replace the chicken with 175g/6oz firm tofu. Cut into cubes, simmer for 5 minutes, then add to the other ingredients.

Chicken Noodle Soup

900ml/1½ pint chicken or vegetable stock (or Miso soup mix)
1 boneless, skinless chicken breast (about 175g/6oz)
1 tsp chopped fresh root ginger
1 garlic clove, finely chopped
50g/2oz rice or wheat noodles
2 tbsp sweetcorn, canned or frozen
2–3 mushrooms, thinly sliced
2 spring onions, shredded
2 tsp soy sauce, plus extra for serving
fresh mint or basil leaves and a little fresh shredded chilli (optional), to serve

Takes 40 minutes • Serves 2

1 Pour the stock into a pan and add the chicken, ginger and garlic. Bring to the boil, then reduce the heat, partly cover and simmer for 20 minutes until the chicken is tender. Remove the chicken to a board and shred into bite-size pieces using a couple of forks.

2 Return the chicken to the stock with the noodles, corn, mushrooms, halve the spring onions and the soy sauce. Simmer for 3–4 minutes until the noodles are tender.

3 Ladle into two bowls and scatter over the remaining spring onions, herbs and chilli shreds, if using. Serve with extra soy sauce for sprinkling.

• Per serving 217 kcalories, protein 26g, carbohydrate 26g, fat 2g, saturated fat 0.4g, fibre 0.6g, added sugar 1g, salt 2.52g

This is such a tasty salad that you'll find it hard to believe it's low fat. It's good with turkey escalopes, too.

Sizzling Pepper Chicken Salad

200g/8oz small new potatoes (Jersey Royals if you can get them), scrubbed and halved
2 celery sticks, sliced diagonally
1 red pepper, seeded and sliced
¼ cucumber, chopped
2 spring onions, finely sliced diagonally
2 small boneless, skinless chicken breasts, total weight about 300g/10oz
1 tsp freshly ground black pepper (more if you like)
1 tbsp olive oil
4 tbsp fat-free Italian-style salad dressing

Takes 25–35 minutes • Serves 2

1 Put the potatoes into a pan of boiling salted water, boil for 8–10 minutes until tender. Drain. Toss the other vegetables in a bowl.
2 Cut the chicken breasts into finger-length strips and toss them with pepper and a little salt to coat them. Heat the olive oil in a frying pan or wok over a medium heat. Tip in the chicken and stir-fry for 4–6 minutes, until golden brown and no longer pink in the middle – cut a piece in half to check.
3 Add the potatoes to the chicken and heat. Pour over the dressing (it will sizzle furiously), and immediately tip the contents of the pan over the vegetables. Toss together and serve.

• Per serving 349 kcalories, protein 40g, carbohydrate 30g, fat 8g, saturated fat 1g, fibre 3g, added sugar none, salt 0.57g

This simple recipe works well
with pork chops, too.

Honeyed Pork with Rosy Apples

1 generous tbsp clear honey
5 tbsp apple juice
2 tbsp chopped fresh sage or
1 rounded tsp dried
1 tsp olive oil
2 pork steaks, about 100g/4oz each,
trimmed of fat
1 red-skinned dessert apple (Empire
are good), cut into 8 wedges
and cored
lemon juice, to taste
boiled rice and green beans,
to serve

Takes 25–35 minutes, plus
marinating time • Serves 2

1 In a non-metallic bowl, mix the honey with the apple juice, sage and oil; season generously. Add the steaks and swish them about until they're coated in the marinade. Leave for 20 minutes.

2 Preheat the grill to medium. Grill the steaks for 3–4 minutes, basting them with the marinade every so often. Toss the apple wedges in the rest of the marinade. Turn the steaks over and tuck the apple wedges in next to them. Grill for another 3–4 minutes until the pork is tender and the apples are turning brown.

3 While the pork and apples are grilling, pour the remaining marinade into a small saucepan and bring to the boil. Simmer until reduced by about a third, season and add lemon juice to your taste. Serve with rice and green beans.

• Per serving 313 kcalories, protein 33g, carbohydrate 25g, fat 10g, saturated fat 2g, fibre 1g, added sugar 11g, salt 0.25g

To make a creamier version, stir 100g/4oz ricotta
or quark into the pasta along with the cooked mushrooms.

Herby Mushroom Pasta

250g/9oz flat or Portobello
mushrooms, thickly sliced
2 tsp wholegrain mustard
3 garlic cloves, sliced or crushed
150ml/¼ pint vegetable stock (from
a cube is fine)
250g/8oz penne pasta (or other tube
shapes)
3 tbsp chopped fresh flatleaf parsley
finely grated zest of 1 lemon

Takes 20 minutes • Serves 2

1 Put the mushrooms, mustard, garlic and
vegetable stock into a frying pan, bring to
the boil and simmer for 5 minutes or until the
stock has nearly all evaporated and the
mushrooms are soft.
2 Meanwhile, cook the pasta according
to the pack instructions.
3 Drain and toss with the mushrooms,
parsley and lemon zest. Season to taste
and serve straight away.

• Per serving 235 kcalories, protein 9g, carbohydrate
49g, fat 2g, saturated fat 0.2g, fibre 3g, added sugar
2g, salt 0.25g

A great quick-and-easy supper dish
using mostly storecupboard ingredients.

Spicy Olive and Tomato Spaghetti

2 tsp olive oil
½ fat fresh red chilli, chopped (leave the seeds in if you like it hot)
1 small garlic clove, chopped
400g can cherry or chopped tomatoes
250g/9oz spaghetti
handful of olives in brine or oil, drained
1–2 tbsp capers, drained
small bunch fresh flatleaf parsley, roughly chopped

Takes 20 minutes • Serves 2

1 Heat the oil in a large frying pan and fry the onion for 5 minutes until softened. Add the chilli and garlic, and cook for another minute. Tip in the tomatoes and leave to bubble for 5 minutes until they start to break up.
2 Meanwhile, cook the spaghetti according to the pack instructions.
3 Stir the olives, capers and half the parsley into the sauce, then fold through the spaghetti. Scatter with the rest of the parsley.

• Per serving 508 kcalories, protein 18g, carbohydrate 98.2g, fat 7.5g, saturated fat 1.1g, fibre 6.6g, added sugar none, salt 2.05g

This creamy risotto makes a delicious backdrop
for sweet, new season peas.

Risotto with Fresh Minted Peas

2 tsp vegetable bouillon powder
(such as Marigold Swiss
vegetable bouillon)
½ tbsp olive oil
1 onion, finely chopped
2 garlic cloves, peeled and finely
chopped
140g/5oz arborio rice
2 tsp lemon juice
175g/6oz fresh or frozen peas,
shelled weight (you will need
450g/1lb peas in their pods)
2 tbsp finely grated vegetarian
parmesan
1 tbsp chopped fresh mint

Takes 30–40 minutes • Serves 2

1 Make the bouillon powder up to 600ml/
1 pint with boiling water for stock. Heat the
oil in a wide, shallow pan and fry the onions
until soft. Add the garlic and rice and cook,
stirring, for a few minutes until the rice turns
translucent. Stir in the lemon juice until most
of the liquid has evaporated.
2 Pour in enough stock to just cover the rice.
Cook, stirring, over a moderate heat for 20
minutes. As the liquid evaporates, gradually
add more stock. When the rice is done,
virtually all the liquid should be absorbed.
3 After the rice has cooked for 15 minutes,
add the peas, bring to a simmer, and cook
for the remaining 5 minutes. Season with
black pepper, stir in three quarters of the
parmesan and mint. Serve scattered with
the remaining cheese and mint.

• Per serving 412 kcalories, protein 16.8g,
carbohydrate 71.8g, fat 8.4g, saturated fat 2.9g,
fibre 6.3g, added sugar none, salt 0.44g

Try this microwave pud idea for a special treat
in just 10 minutes.

Maple Pears with Cranberries

2 ripe pears
small handful of dried cranberries
1 tbsp maple syrup, plus extra
to serve
25g/1oz pecan nuts, roughly broken
Greek yogurt, to serve

Takes 10 minutes • Serves 2

1 Peel and halve the pears and scoop out the cores with a teaspoon. Lay the halves in a shallow microwaveable dish, cut side down, along with the cranberries. Pour 1 tablespoon of the maple syrup over and cover with cling film.
2 Microwave on High for 3 minutes until softened, stirring halfway through. Uncover and leave to cool for a few minutes. Stir the pecan nuts through the syrup.
3 Spoon into serving dishes, drizzle extra maple syrup over, if you like, and serve with yogurt.

• Per serving 193 kcalories, protein 1.6g, carbohydrate 27.9g, fat 9.1g, saturated fat 0.8g, fibre 4.2g, added sugar 4.6, salt 0.02g

Turn a tub of ice cream
into an indulgent treat.

Strawberry Mess

200g/8oz strawberries
1 ready-made meringue nest
scoops of strawberry ice cream

Takes 10 minutes • Serves 2

1 Hull the strawberries. Roughly mash half of them with a fork and slice the rest.
2 Divide the strawberries between two bowls.
3 Break the meringue nest into rough pieces, than scatter over the strawberries. Top with scoops of ice cream.

• Per serving 197 kcalories, protein 3.9g, carbohydrate 32.7g, fat 6.5g, saturated fat 4.3g, fibre 1.1g, added sugar 20g, salt 0.16g

For a special occasion, add a dash of vodka
to the syrup before pouring over the fruit.

Raspberry and Mango Salad

100ml/3½oz cranberry juice
1½ tsp caster sugar
1 medium ripe mango
150g punnet raspberries
vanilla ice cream or yogurt,
to serve

Takes 10 minutes • Serves 2

1 In a small pan, bring the cranberry juice and sugar to a rolling boil, then remove from the heat and leave to cool.

2 Meanwhile, peel and thinly slice the mango, then tip into a large bowl with the raspberries.

3 Pour the cranberry syrup over, then spoon into bowls. Serve with scoops of ice cream or spoonfuls of yogurt.

• Per serving 142 kcalories, protein 2.1g, carbohydrate 34.4g, fat 0.5g, saturated fat none, fibre 5.8g, added sugar 8.3g, salt 0.03g

Use good-quality vanilla ice cream to make the most of this oozingly delicious chocolate dessert.

Choc-mel Muffins

50g chocolate caramel bar
2 tbsp double cream
2 chocolate muffins
4 scoops of vanilla ice cream

Takes 10 minutes • Serves 2

1 Break the chocolate bar in pieces into a small pan. Spoon in the cream and heat gently, stirring over a low heat until just melted.

2 Scoop a little bit from the middle of each muffin to make a small hole.

3 Drop a couple of scoops of ice cream onto each muffin, then drizzle the chocolate sauce over the top.

• Per serving 486 kcalories, protein 6.7g, carbohydrate 52.3g, fat 29.3g, saturated fat 16.1g, fibre 0.6g, added sugar 38.8g, salt 0.43g

Perfect served with a glass of Asti Spumante
at the end of a summer meal.

Chocolate Berry Cups

148ml carton double cream
50g/2oz dark chocolate, broken into
pieces
1 tbsp icing sugar
280g/10oz mixed summer fruits
(raspberries, strawberries,
cherries, blueberries), stoned and
halved if necessary

Takes 15–20 minutes • Serves 2

1 Heat the cream in a saucepan until just coming to the boil. Remove from the heat, drop in the chocolate pieces, then stir until melted. Cool slightly.

2 Tip the icing sugar and most of the fruit into the pan and mix gently.

3 Spoon into two glasses or cups, top with the remaining fruit, then chill in the fridge until needed (up to 3 hours ahead of serving).

• Per serving 580 kcalories, protein 3.8g, carbohydrate 37.6g, fat 47g, saturated fat 26.3g, fibre 3.7g, added sugar 28.6g, salt 0.06g

This fresh and tasty smoothie tastes best if the berries are chilled, so put them in the fridge overnight.

Breakfast Smoothie

2 small ripe bananas
about 300g/10oz blackberries, blueberries, raspberries or strawberries (or use a mix), plus extra to serve
apple juice or mineral water (optional)
runny honey, to serve

Takes 5 minutes • Serves 2

1 Slice the banana into your blender or food processor and add the berries of your choice. Whizz until smooth.
2 With the blades whirring, pour in enough juice or water to make the consistency you like.
3 Toss a few extra fruits on top, drizzle with honey and serve.

• Per serving 115 kcalories, protein 2.3g, carbohydrate 27g, fat 0.5g, saturated fat 0.1g, fibre 4.1g, added sugar none, salt 0.02g

Strawberries make the easiest daiquiries
because they blend really smoothly.

Berry Daiquiri

350g/12oz ripe strawberries or
400g/14oz raspberries (or use
a mix of 200g/8oz strawberries
and 200g/8oz raspberries)
about 12 ice cubes
juice of 1 lime
2 tbsp lemon juice
200ml/7floz white rum
2 small lime slices, to serve

Takes 10 minutes • Serves 2

1 If using raspberries, blend these first to
a purée then rub through a sieve to extract
the pips.
2 Put a handful of ice cubes in a powerful
blender and crush. Add the berries or pulp,
plus the lime and lemon juice and rum.
3 Whizz again and pour into two chilled
cocktail glasses straight away. Decorate
each with a lime slice.

• Per serving 271 kcalories, protein 1.5g,
carbohydrate 10.9g, fat 0.2g, saturated fat none,
fibre 2g, added sugar none, salt 0.03g

Prepare this exquisite puds up to 4 hours ahead and keep in the fridge.
If cooking from cold, give them an extra 2–3 minutes in the oven.

Valentine's Molten Chocolate Pots

50g/2oz butter, plus extra for
greasing
1 tbsp ground almonds, plus extra
for dusting
100g/4oz dark chocolate, broken in
pieces
1 medium egg yolk
1 medium egg
2 tbsp golden caster sugar
4 tbsp Baileys
icing sugar to dust

Takes 25–30 minutes • Serves 2

1 Preheat oven to 230°C/Gas 8/fan oven
210°C. Make the stencils by up-ending a
ramekin or coffee cup (whichever you are
using) and tracing a circle around it onto
paper. Draw a smaller heart shape within the
circle. Cut out the circle, then cut the heart
from it, to make two stencils.
Butter two large ramekins or heatproof coffee
cups and dust with ground almonds. Melt the
chocolate and butter together.
2 Whisk the yolk, whole egg and sugar until
light and pale then gently fold in the
chocolate-butter mixture, ground almonds and
Baileys. Divide between the ramekins. Bake
for 10 minutes until puffed up and just set.
3 Place a stencil over each cooked pudding.
Dust the puddings with icing sugar, remove
the paper and serve immediately.

• Per serving 735 kcalories, protein 9g, carbohydrate
60g, fat 50g, saturated fat 23g, fibre 2g, added sugar
58g, salt 0.66g

This tasty pud is the perfect end
to an exotic feast.

Hot Passion Pina Coladas

1 passion fruit
2 slices of fresh pineapple
icing sugar, to coat
4 tsp rum or Malibu
2 big scoops of coconut ice cream

Takes 15 minutes • Serves 2

1 Halve the passion fruit and scoop out the pulp. Set aside.
2 Coat the pineapple slices in icing sugar. Heat a small non-stick heavy-based frying pan, add the pineapple slices and cook for a few minutes until caramelised on each side, turning once.
3 Lay each pineapple slice on a plate, drizzle with the rum or Malibu, then top with scoops of the ice cream. Spoon the passion fruit pulp over and serve.

• Per serving 233 kcalories, protein 2.9g, carbohydrate 32.8g, fat 8.5g, saturated fat 6g, fibre 1.6g, added sugar 22.8g, salt 0.11g

The fragrance of the basil works really well with the scented peaches in this special, easy and low-fat dessert.

Warm Peaches with Basil and Honey

knob of unsalted butter
1 ripe peach or nectarine, stoned and thickly sliced
1 tbsp clear honey
juice of ½ orange
4–5 fresh basil leaves, shredded
vanilla or white chocolate ice cream, to serve

Takes 10 minutes • Serves 2

1 Melt the butter in a frying pan, add the peach or nectarine slices, then cook on both sides until slightly softened (about 3 minutes).
2 Add the honey and stir to make a sauce, then pour in the orange juice and allow to bubble briefly.
3 Stir in the basil and serve warm with scoops of ice cream.

• Per serving 76 kcalories, protein 0.7g, carbohydrate 11.4g, fat 3.3g, saturated fat 2.1g, fibre 0.8g, added sugar 5.7g, salt 0.01g

Splash a few tablespoons of armagnac or brandy over the figs
before grilling to make a boozy pudding.

Sticky Cinnamon Figs

4 ripe figs
knob of butter
2 tbsp clear honey
small handful of shelled pistachio
nuts or almonds
½ tsp ground cinnamon or mixed
spice
mascarpone or Greek yogurt,
to serve

Takes 10 minutes • Serves 2

1 Preheat a grill to medium-high. Cut a deep cross in the top of each fig, then ease the top apart so it opens like a flower.
2 Sit the figs in a small baking dish and drop a piece of butter into the centre of each fruit. Drizzle the honey over the figs, then sprinkle with the nuts and spice.
3 Grill for 5 minutes until the figs are softened and the honey and butter make a sticky sauce in the bottom of the dish. Serve warm with dollops of mascarpone or yogurt.

• Per serving 186 kcalories, protein 3.6g, carbohydrate 24.1g, fat 9.1g, saturated fat 2.8g, fibre 1.7g, added sugar 11.5g, salt 0.08g

This easy idea will get you out of a
dessert dilemma in minutes.

Cookie Ice Cream Sandwiches

8 chocolate chip cookies
scoops of slightly softened
good-quality vanilla or chocolate
ice cream
handful of blueberries and
raspberries

Takes 5 minutes • Serves 2

1 Sandwich the cookies together with the ice cream.
2 Tuck a few blueberries and raspberries between each.
3 Return to the freezer to eat later, or eat straight away.

• Per serving 298 kcalories, protein 4.8g, carbohydrate 37.7g, fat 15.2g, saturated fat 5.2g, fibre 0.9g, added sugar 22.6g, salt 0.41g

In mid-summer, try using fresh berries rather than frozen.

Iced Summer Berries with White Chocolate Sauce

200g/4oz mixed frozen berries, such as raspberries, blueberries, strawberries (or fresh)

FOR THE SAUCE
½ × 142ml carton double cream
85g/3oz white chocolate

Takes 5 minutes • Serves 2

1 Let the frozen berries thaw slightly – they should be icy but not solidly frozen. (If using fresh berries, freeze briefly until they are icy, but not solid.)
2 Make the sauce. Pour the cream into a small pan and break in the chocolate. Heat gently, stirring, until the chocolate melts and the sauce is smooth. If the heat gets too high, the chocolate will seize.
3 Pile the berries into shallow dishes and pour the hot chocolate sauce over, so they start to soften in the warmth of the sauce.

• Per serving 609 kcalories, protein 5.4g, carbohydrate 33.1g, fat 51.5g, saturated fat 29.2g, fibre 2.7g, added sugar 20.2g, salt 0.19g

Impress your guests with this sensational dessert –
a real special-occasion pudding.

Tropical Crème Brûlées

½ medium ripe mango
1 passion fruit
½ × 200ml carton crème fraîche
1 tsp rum
2 scant tbsp golden caster sugar

Takes 10–15 minutes • Serves 2

1 Peel the mango, cut the flesh into small chunks and divide evenly between two 175ml/6fl oz ramekin dishes. Halve the passion fruit and scoop the contents of each half over the mango.
2 Mix the crème fraîche and rum together and spoon over the fruit to cover. Chill well.
3 To serve, sprinkle a spoonful of the sugar over the top of each dish and brûlée until the sugar has caramelised. This is best done with a blowtorch, as it is hard to get them to caramelise under a grill. Leave for about 5 minutes to harden before serving. (If you don't have a blowtorch, just sprinkle the tops with dark muscovado sugar and leave for about 10 minutes for the sugar to dissolve and give a brulée look.)

• Per serving 289 kcalories, protein 1.8g, carbohydrate 25.3g, fat 20.2g, saturated fat 12.9g, fibre 2.2g, added sugar 13.1g, salt 0.04g

Index

Picture credits and recipe credits

BBC Worldwide would like to thank the following for providing photographs. While every effort has been made to trace and acknowledge all photographers, we would like to apologize should there be any errors or omissions.

Marie-Louise Avery p47, p63, p119; Iain Bagwell p109, p147; Steve Baxter p27, p61, p87, p145, p155, p183, p189; Peter Cassidy p125, p187, p191, p201; Ken Field p21, p29, p33, p35, p37, p45, p51, p59, p71, p115, p143, p153, p161; Gus Filgate p105, p199; Will Heap p25, p49, p57, p181, p205; Lisa Linder p193; William Lingwood p13, p23, p41, p139; David Munns p11, p19, p79, p101, p113, p129, p131, p169, p173, p203, p209; Myles New p207; Michael Paul p53, p149, p157; Myles New & Craig Robertson p165; Craig Robertson p85, p123, p163, p179, p185, p211; Roger Stowell p55, p95, p97, p103, p111, p135, p137, p141, p158; Simon Walton p69, p89, p93, p175, p177; Cameron Watt p39, p67, p91, p121, p127, p133, p171; Philip Webb p31, p43, p65, p73, p81, p83, p117, p167, p195, p197; Simon Wheeler p75, p77, p107, p151; Geoff Wilkinson p17; Peter Williams p15, p99.

The recipes in this book have been created by the editorial team on *BBC Good Food Magazine* and regular contributors to the magazine.